METAPHYSICAL TECHNIQUES
THAT REALLY WORK

Metaphysical Techniques
That Really Work

Audrey Craft Davis

Additional copies of **Metaphysical Techniques That Really Work** are available by mail for $12.95 each. Send check or money order plus $2.00 postage and handling to: **Valley of the Sun Publishing,** Box 38, Malibu, California 90265. A catalog of over 300 tapes and books is also available. Write for more information.

Printed in the United States of America
First Printing: March 1996
Valley of the Sun Publishing, Box 38, Malibu, CA 90265

ISBN: 0-87554-597-1
Library of Congress Card Number: 95-062220

Dedication

To my wonderful husband, Louis, who without his under-standing, assistance and faith, this book might not have been written. To my friend and computer technician John Meyers, for his undying patience and belief in me. To my daughter, Alice Schuler, my son James V. Craft, my loving sister, Minnie Beam and especially, to my late mother, who taught me true values and how to believe in myself. To my deceased brother Jim, who came back many times as he promised, to confirm there is life after death.

Contents

INTRODUCTION

Metaphysical Techniques That Really Work

What is Metaphysics? When translated from the Greek words *meta,* meaning "after," and *physika,* meaning "the physical," metaphysics literally means "higher and beyond the physical." Merriam Webster's dictionary defines the word as "abstract philosophical studies, a study of what is outside objective experience."

I prefer to define metaphysics as a natural mind science—the science of being—and the true language of the soul in its dialogue between Divine and human nature.

Metaphysical Techniques That Really Work will guide you in the unfoldment of your higher spiritual and mental potential, and teach you how to improve your life and gain command of your world. You will learn to control invisible influences and to achieve the seemingly impossible through the use of these powerful spiritual techniques, which are based upon the appropriate use of universal laws.

In **Chapter One**, you will see that your thoughts have

made you what you are today. You will learn treasure-mapping techniques that can help you achieve what you may now consider to be impossible. Examples and techniques are given that will lead you step by step to the realization of your most cherished dreams. The power of thought is so awesome that it can change the course of civilization. Collective thoughts have a tremendous effect on our planet. Did you know that, by the way you think, you are not only creating your present world but also the one which you will inherit in your next life?

The Bible, the Koran, the Bhagavad-Gita, and other holy books and scriptures admit to knowledge of spirits and angels. Everyone has a guardian angel—are you in touch with yours? In **Chapter Two**, you will learn an easy technique to initiate contact with and receive guidance from your angel. You'll also read exciting accounts of actual happenings in which guardian angels have performed impossible feats. This chapter also tells of ghosts and of my own experiences while living in a house haunted by earthbound spirits.

Chapter Three introduces you to your very own, personal genie who will never question your judgment and who never sleeps. This genie can bring you miraculous power to achieve your greatest desires. This same genie, when misdirected, can cause as much grief as pleasure. You will learn techniques to tap the power of your subconscious mind and bring this obedient servant under your control.

Did you know that a person can be in two different places at the same time? In **Chapter Four**, you will read examples of sages who have done so, as well as examples of ordinary people who have experienced this phenomenon known as bi-location. You will learn a simple astral projection technique that will enable you to release yourself from your physical body and soar in spirit to any destination you choose. You will learn that this body, which you consider to be your "self," is not the *real* you! Once you have mastered this technique, you will never again fear the seeming separation of death; instead you will recognize it as part of the eternal growth and change cycle.

In **Chapter Five**, you will learn a metaphysical technique that boosts mental, physical and spiritual energy almost immediately and lasts for hours. It is so powerful that you must do this exercise *only* in early morning; otherwise you will have so much energy, you will not be able to sleep that night!

Do you know the power of numbers? For example, did you know that the number thirteen is the luckiest of all numbers? Many think thirteen is an unlucky omen or the symbol of death. Instead, thirteen represents life and attainment through regeneration, signifying completeness or infinity. Additionally, thirteen is a "holy" number which cannot be divided. In **Chapter Six**, you will find that numbers were here before letters. This is why letters have a numerical value. Numbers can tell you much about your life as well as others. What kind of day and year will you have? Have you ever wondered if you and your mate are compatible? This chapter offers a do-it-yourself technique that will teach you how to find the answers.

Is it my right to prosper? **Chapter Seven** will show you that it is not a virtue to be poor nor a vice to be rich. Indeed, it is your duty to prosper. This chapter teaches you how. I have known thirteen millionaires who obtained their wealth through the use of metaphysical laws yet not one of them was familiar with the term "metaphysics." Each one accidently set the metaphysical law of prosperity into action and reaped the harvest of abundance without knowing how they did it. I have also seen many people at the other end of the scale, who used metaphysical laws to remain forever poor.

Chapter Eight will show you how to build a priceless energy power, and teach you how to store and use this power to benefit yourself and the planet. This is the subtle force used in many psychic gifts, such as astral projection, precognition, levitation, psychometry, as well as healing and protection. You will also learn techniques to read, strengthen and heal your aura and those of your loved ones.

Did you know that the astral body can be healed, thereby producing the same effect as in the physical body? In **Chapter Nine** you will learn a scientific healing technique that you can use to benefit yourself and others. Learn that all healing is divine, whether laying on of hands, surgery, medication, or natural instinct!

Have we lived before? **Chapter Ten** says we certainly have, probably many lifetimes! The people who are in your life now were probably with you in other lives. Would you like to discover who you were in another life? Learn a simple technique that requires no hypnosis or regression.

Learn the mysteries of the other side in **Chapter Eleven**. It is filled with actual spine-tingling mystical happenings and simple techniques you can use to communicate with the spirits of departed loved ones.

You will note that in most chapters, I describe the technique, then at the end of the chapter, I again repeat it. This is done for a purpose. First, you become familiar with the technique by reading about it, then at the end of the chapter you follow the step-by-step instructions to actually use the technique and incorporate it into your life.

As with any deep subject matter, the more one learns,

the more there is to learn. It took several years of college to earn my degrees in Metaphysics, Psychology and Divinity. Einstein once said, "If I could live for a thousand years, perhaps I could learn something!"

Metaphysics is not a destination, but rather a lifelong journey. The universal laws of metaphysics exact their recompense in accordance to our knowledge of how to use them. Ignorance of these basic metaphysical laws does not exempt one from their consequences, whether it be good or bad! We cannot change the laws. What we can do is learn how to use them not only for our own welfare but that of everyone on the planet.

AUDREY CRAFT DAVIS

CHAPTER ONE

Thoughts & Treasure Mapping

Words and Thoughts are Things

The power of thought is the highest power in the universe. It is the product of the process of thinking, which includes learning, developing concepts, memory, creativity, communication, using words, abstracting, insight, intuiting, logic, problem solving, rationality and anticipating the future. It is this mental vibration that is at the heart of our creative center, enabling us to be co-creators of the manifestations in our lives.

All force or power is derived from thought. The power of thought is transmitted from mind to mind and from mind to body in all living beings. Thoughts work with other thoughts throughout all infinity. Thought is so powerful that the force of one thought can change the course of a civilization, yet no one knows exactly what thought is. Despite the great strides science has made toward a model of how the brain works, science still cannot analyze a thought nor dissect it in a laboratory nor view it through a microscope.

The Universal Law of thought says that the mental activity of the physical kingdom directs the course of the very atoms of the universe to make three-dimensional manifestations. In other words, every thought that goes forth from the brain sends vibrations into the atmosphere; the intensity of the concentration of the thinker determines the effect. This Universal Law functions because of other Universal Laws, including the Universal Law of like attracts like. We become either a negative or a positive pole, depending on the direction of our thoughts.

If you project angry, resentful, hateful thoughts, you'll attract harmful energies to yourself. If you send out positive, loving energy, you'll invite the same kind of thoughts and feelings. Negative thoughts build a discordant atmosphere while positive ones produce harmony. Free will gives us the choice to think positively or negatively—we can accept or reject a thought! Fervently do I wish I had known this earlier in my life. We build our world by the thoughts we think ... your very thoughts are not only creating your present world but also the one which you will inherit in your next life. Our mental activity directs the course of the universe; it is this thought energy that holds the world together. Metaphysician Emmet Fox said, "Everything manifested in earth is the mental equivalent of the thoughts of every man in earth." Elmer Green said it even more simply: "The world is crystallized thought."

Positive collective thought can produce healing and peace. The sages of old knew this. They had large groups of people to chant and do mantras. They believed that collective thoughts and words band together and set off vibrations within the universe. If these vibrations are positive in nature, the resulting effect can be very beneficial, contributing to peace and harmony on our planet. The reverse is also true—collective thought can cause disastrous results if it is negative. Examples of this are war, poverty and famine.

An example of collective thought power can be found in the old adage, "The rich get richer and the poor get poorer." The wealthy man is so busy thinking of his next million that his very thoughts form a collective affirmation of his wealth. The poor man contributes with his thoughts of how the rich get richer while he dwells on his poverty.

Words and thoughts are things, they materialize. The old adage, "What the mind of man can conceive and believe, it can achieve," is proven daily in almost every field of human endeavor. We often set a situation in motion by our thinking. I had a thought, "I must not spill this." I dropped it, almost as if I had planned it. Why? Our subconscious does not hear negative words; it only hears commands for action. The picture in my mind was of spilling the milk. It was what I was trying to avoid, but it's exactly what I was visualizing. What my subconscious heard was "I must spill this" instead of "I must **not** spill this." Naturally, I dropped the drink as my subconscious mind tried to fulfill the expressed desire it had heard.

Another example of this was related to me by a friend. She told me how her husband had flown their Piper Cub hundreds of times without incident until one day he expressed his concern at the breakfast table. Looking out the window, he said, "Look at that fence. If I ever came in a little too low, it could be disastrous!" Sure enough, the very next time he flew their plane, he came in a little too low and ripped off a wing! Of course, he had set that up by voicing the desire to his subconscious, which fulfilled his wishes. We should not think or voice a negative even to denounce it!

How often do we think of another only to have them call? Many million dollar businesses are not the idea of the owner. Often it is the result of that person picking up the thoughts of another who lacked the resources or the courage to follow through, on his own idea.

We are the captain of our own ship. Our building blocks are our thoughts and since they produce after their own kind, we must learn to ignore negative thoughts. Have you ever noticed that if you think of one characteristic which you dislike in a person, soon you will be wondering why you ever saw any good in him? Conversely, love is blind; we see only the good which attracts like thoughts.

Recently a friend thrust his negativity into my otherwise beautiful world. By the time I listened to his troubles, my own space was discordant. I found myself resenting his intrusion. Oh, yes, I wanted to help by listening but I let it momentarily disturb my peace of mind. Then I remembered that we do have control over our thoughts. It was my own decision to let his negativity invade my thoughts. I could blame no one but myself.

To achieve the results you desire, you must learn to think in a new way. Mere wishful thinking is not enough to use the universal laws properly and may only incompletely or even inappropriately fulfill your desires. Learning to control our thoughts is one of the most important lessons we can learn. Our thoughts travel through the ethers much like radio waves, ready to be picked up by others. Science concurs that every thought and every word ever spoken is still alive, in space. Our thoughts are a bridge to other worlds.

Before you begin this exercise, rid your mind of all

negativity. Clear your space. Then drop an invisible shield around yourself. Imagine that only those thoughts and circumstances of a positive nature can penetrate this shield. Visualize a golden cord attached to the forehead reaching out into infinity opening up vistas of Cosmic Mind. Imagine this divine essence flowing into your mind. Next, visualize the kind of world you would like to live in. Think thoughts of abundance, beauty and harmony to enrich your own world as well as to uplift the vibration of the planet.

It has been said, "Every thought is a prayer." What are we praying for at this moment? We often open the door to unclean spirits by our thoughts. Let us think only those thoughts which we wish to have reproduced in our world and in the lives of those we love. Then we will be opening the door, where only spirits of love and beneficence abound.

Treasure Mapping

Treasure-mapping is a form of prayer. It requires more faith than the usual way of praying and is scientific in design. In treasure-mapping, we are giving the Divine Source a concise picture of what we desire. In metaphysics, we often use the words "treating for" something.

Your subconscious mind is the direct channel to Universal Mind; your means of fulfilling your dreams. When we pray for something we have a picture in our subconscious mind of exactly what we desire. But nothing can happen until our conscious and our subconscious minds are in agreement. Treasure-mapping does this.

Our conscious mind governs all our senses. It questions and reasons; wants everything to be logical. So when you ask for a new car and you have no cash nor credit, your conscious mind says, "It is not logical. It cannot happen!"

When we show our conscious mind a picture, we are stimulating some or maybe all of our senses—sight, hearing, touch, and sometimes even taste and smell. We want the conscious mind to see the same picture as the subconscious, to avoid conflict of purpose.

The scripture states, "Prove me now and I'll open up the windows of heaven and pour you out a blessing so big you can't contain it." What is meant by; prove me? We must believe so sincerely that The Divine will answer our prayers; the very desires of our heart that we are willing to sign a contract. That takes commitment!

The technique: Select a picture of what you desire from a magazine or an ad and put it on a poster or in a book. I use a photograph album. This way, I can easily remove the picture when it has materialized. I know I must remove it almost immediately unless I want more than one.

Always write, "This or something better, Creator" and sign your name. Remember when you sign your name, you are making a contract. Be very sure that you really want whatever the picture portrays. When you look at the picture, feel the exhilaration as if you already own the object. Be enthusiastic! The following statement is one of the most important things you will ever learn to make your dreams a reality. So memorize it. *Your subconscious does not know the difference between a real and an imagined experience*.

The best time to practice your visualization is just before going to sleep and upon awakening. Notice that as you are feeling drowsy, your senses are dormant. At this time and while you sleep, your subconscious mind has full control, with no opposition from the logical, conscious mind. Your subconscious never sleeps. It is on the job twenty-four hours a day and is 90 to 95 percent more powerful than your conscious mind.

When you are looking at your picture and feeling as though you actually own the object it portrays, your subconscious mind believes it is true. Remember, *your subconscious mind does not know the difference between a real and an imaginary experience.* It merely sees what you want and sets about making it happen. Since the mind sees in pictures, it can only work with the picture you give it. Your subconscious is your direct access to the Creator and has no choice but to actualize your picture.

There is a good reason for writing, "This or something better." He knows better than you what is good for you. You might desire a Cadillac and the Creator might want you to have a Rolls Royce.

I remember when my husband and I were treating for a larger condo. We thought we knew what we wanted. We didn't get that particular one but rather, one just like it. The builder of the condo we thought we wanted was having financial difficulties and we didn't know it. It was a good thing we wrote, "This or something better," for the Creator knew of the problem. We now own one just like it but with no financial difficulties.

It is important to know the difference between the meaning of objective and subjective. You are being objective when you are looking at something outside yourself, like a picture. The beta brain wave frequency (your ordinary waking consciousness) is objective.

The subjective subconscious is associated with the alpha brain wave frequency, which is 90-95 percent more powerful than the objective, conscious mind. While in the subjective mode, you are in the picture. You are living the experience of owning the thing you desire.

As an example, being world travelers, my husband and I

can watch a TV program about a place we have visited. We can put ourselves into the picture and can re-experience the excitement. This is subjective.

Now the picture changes to a place we have never been. In this instance we are looking at the picture. We are not in it. This is objective. See the difference?

If you are treasure-mapping for a new house, you should actually find the house of your dreams and go inside. Get the feeling that you own this very house. This puts you in the picture, looking out, not on the outside looking in.

The more you can become part of the picture, the faster it will materialize, as you will see in the true story of how Doris' visualization of a new car happened almost overnight. She became part of the picture. Follow the steps and see how her action was subjective.

But first a little more instruction. Each time you look at your picture and do your visualization, you are reaffirming your goal. Do this at night. It is most important to go to sleep with the feeling that you already are in possession of the thing for which you are treasure-mapping. Your subconscious mind will use this picture to materialize your desire. Remember, *your subconscious mind does not know the difference between a real and an imaginary experience.*

When doing this visualization during the day, it is necessary to immediately release the picture when you have finished the exercise. Scrub the floor, rake the leaves; do anything that requires conscious effort. Keep this logical, reasoning part of your mind busy! Do not allow yourself to think about your dream until the next time you deliberately do this exercise.

Remember that treasure-mapping is neither logical nor reasonable since you are asking for things which are beyond your normal range of obtaining. Treasure-mapping is subconscious activity.

It is most important that you have a complete picture in your mind. If it is a car you want, you must know the color inside and out, what make and model; is it a two-door? Does it have bucket seats? Do you know how it feels to drive this car? You must get the feeling that you own this car. Here is the story of Doris's treasure-mapping experience.

Doris's battered Ford chugged to a halt in my driveway.

"Doris," I exclaimed, "You need a new car!"

"Yeah, tell me about it! But there is no way I can get a new car. I barely make ends meet as it is!" Doris sighed.

"You're right. I couldn't agree more. As long as you think you can't, you can't! That is faith and it works!" I said.

"What do you mean, that's faith? I thought faith was just something you believe," Doris said, tilting her head to one side and eyeing me quizzically.

"Doris, have you ever heard of negative faith?" I asked.

As if slightly amused, she answered, "No, tell me about negative faith."

"Negative faith is believing you can't do something or have a certain thing. Didn't you just now say there's no way you could have a new car?" I asked.

"I thought all I did was tell the truth," she said.

"The truth as your limited consciousness sees it. I can show you how to get a new car. If you will do exactly as I instruct you, I will even guarantee it!" I told her.

Leaning on her beat-up jalopy, she answered, "Honey, with you guaranteeing it, how can I lose? Let's get started!"

"Do you have a picture of the car you would most like to own?" I asked.

"You bet I do! I knew it was stupid but I pretended that

I was going to buy a Toyota Corolla, just to get a chance to drive it!" She answered.

"How did it feel to drive that car?" I asked.

Flinging her arms over her head, she quipped, "It was absolute heaven!"

"Hold that feeling! This is the emotion I want you to have every time you look at the picture of your car. You did say you have a picture of it, didn't you?"

"Of course, I do. I have it under my pillow. Silly, huh?"

"No," I answered, "It is not silly. You are going to use that picture to possess your car. You are going to treasure-map for it."

"I'm going to do what? What on earth is treasure-mapping?" Doris asked.

I had her put the picture on a poster and write on the bottom, "This or something better, Creator" and then sign her name. She was instructed to look at the picture often, especially when going to sleep and upon rising.

She was instructed to feel exuberant every time she saw the picture—to feel as though she already owned the car. If a negative thought intruded, she was to say with fervor, "Cancel!"

At seven a.m. two days later, my phone was ringing off the hook. I knew it was Doris.

"Guess what? You won't believe what I'm about to tell you!"

"The Toyota is in your driveway, right?" I answered.

"How could you possibly know?" she inquired.

I answered, "The way you were following the formula, it had to work! There was no way it could not."

She couldn't wait to fill me in on the details. It seems she didn't waste any time. After I gave her the instructions, the very next day, she went back to the dealer to look at her dream car. "I thought I'd die," she said, "The car was gone!"

Grabbing a salesman by the sleeve, she almost screamed, "Where is that blue Toyota Corolla?"

"I'm sorry, ma'am, we sold it yesterday!"

"You have another one just like it, huh?" she asked.

"No, ma'am, we don't and I know we don't have any on order. I am sorry." Dejectedly, Doris started walking toward her dilapidated Ford when Bob, her companion, called out to her. "Doris, come here!"

The salesman walked over to Bob, "Fella, I know you mean well, but don't get her hopes up. The lot you are staring at is only for big cars. We would never put a small or midsize car over there."

Ignoring the salesman, Bob proceeded toward a spot of blue, peeking out from behind some big cars. He yelled, again, "Doris, I have found your car!"

There it was. An exact replica of her dream car. But they could see the front seats had been slashed—vandalized.

Heading straight for the manager's office, Doris was determined to find a way to possess that car. She reasoned, she could put seat covers on it.

"What are you planning to do with that vandalized Toyota Corolla?" she asked.

"We have to ship it back to the factory and have new seats installed," he answered.

"Couldn't you reduce it by that amount? Wouldn't you rather sell it? If you can make it affordable to me, I'll buy it," she said, straightening her shoulders, trying to appear confident.

After making several phone calls, he decided to let Doris have the car and even made the payments fit her limited budget.

Today, Doris has no doubt that "seeing is believing."

I have a separate album which I use for intangibles. In it, I put phrases, typewritten or cut from inspirational literature, for qualities I would like to acquire, like being kinder, more loving; for having good mental and physical health. I add pictures that depict these qualities. I sometimes put in pictures of my loved ones with appropriate phrases. When wanting to lose a few pounds, it is good to find a picture of yourself when you were your ideal size with an appropriate caption underneath. If you don't have such a picture, find a picture of someone who is the ideal size, and replace the model's face with your own.

We treasure-map in our minds all the time for we cannot think without putting a picture there. Beware of what the picture portrays. Make sure it is one you will want to materialize!

In these techniques, you may use the words Universal Intelligence, The All That Is, The Divine, Cosmic Consciousness, or whatever you prefer.

Treasure Mapping Technique

1. Have a complete mental picture of what you want, down to the tiniest detail.

2. Paste a picture of the item on a poster or in a book.

3. Write on the bottom of the picture, "This or something better. Thank you, Creator." Use any name you like, Universal Intelligence or Divine Source, whatever makes you comfortable.

4. Sign your name with the realization that you are signing a contract.

5. Look at your picture often with the emotion of excitement which goes with ownership. Claim it now! Remember, *your subconscious mind does not know the difference between a real and an imaginary experience.*

6. Accept it and give thanks.

7. As soon as your dream has materialized, remove that picture and replace it with a picture of something else you desire for yourself or for someone else.

AUDREY CRAFT DAVIS

CHAPTER TWO

. . . .

Different Kinds of Spirits

Everyone has guardian angels, spirit guides, celestial guardians, or whatever you choose to call them. Most religions of the world identify spirit guides or angels in their teachings. In ancient Greece, an angel was referred to as a *daimon*. In Eastern religions, such an etheric being is referred to as an *Avatar, Gandharva* or *Deva*. Mohammed speaks of angels in the Muslim scriptures. Angels are recognized in the Bhagavad Gita and the Koran. The Bible refers to angels (spirits) in 113 scriptures.

These spirits are advanced beings, soul-minds in the etheric world, to be loved and appreciated, but only the Divine Presence is to be worshipped. These beings have lived innumerable lives on the earth plane and have chosen or earned the right to help humans in their souls' evolution. Messengers of the inner light, their purpose is to arouse the higher faculties, to administer guidance, protection, assistance, psychic information and hidden information to those they serve. These beings do not make choices for us, but they do offer guidance when it is sought.

A person may have several of these angels or spirit guides. Some remain with one individual for that person's entire lifetime; others may be drawn to the individual only for a period of time when they can be of assistance. We should call on them often. Only in this way, can they fulfill their purpose on earth.

I have seen my spirit guides and my husband has seen them. They have been with me all my life.

Recently, I dozed off with one of my legs hanging off the bed. I awakened as I felt a hand pick up my leg and tenderly place it back upon the bed. I thought, "How sweet of my husband" but as I opened my eyes, I found him fast asleep. I knew then, it had been my spirit guide.

The technique: You can get to know your spirit guides or guardian angels. Go to a quiet room and relax your physical body and conscious self, and allow your mind to release its cares. Light a candle. Stare into the candle until you see your spirit guide enter the area where you are. Tell them that you know they are there. Then, ask them to do something for you or someone you love. In the beginning, it is wise to do this as you are getting ready to go to sleep, just before dozing off. This is the best time to reach them, while the conscious, reasoning mind is dormant.

Encounters With Guardian Angels

After you become familiar with your guardian angels (spirit guides) and learn to trust them and their guidance, they may appear without being summoned, as demonstrated in the following incident.

A friend told me of an experience with her guardian

angel that occurred while she and her husband were moving into their new home. The move was going well until Fred started moving the refrigerator. He had gotten it from the truck to the house when he became trapped between the doorway and the refrigerator. She rushed to his aid, and though she tried with all her strength, she could not budge the refrigerator. It was slowly crushing Fred against the doorway and he began to have difficulty breathing.

She stared at him in panic, not knowing what to do. She sent a despairing mental cry for help heavenward. Then, "I swear to you," she said, "a large, muscular man appeared out of nowhere, picked up that fridge with no effort at all, carried it into the kitchen and placed it exactly where I had planned to put it. Then he vanished as quickly as he had appeared, never saying a word."

Another occasion of guardian angel assistance involved my sister. She had been in two sequential automobile accidents which had seriously damaged the nerves in her neck, head and brain. Not knowing that sonic waves could affect her condition, she boarded a plane and came from Ohio to Florida to visit me. This required her to change planes, both coming and returning. Each time the plane took off and landed, the changes in the sonic frequencies nearly killed her!

When I met her in the terminal, I was shocked. My beautiful sister's face was distorted in pain and she was stooped over like an old lady. I could scarcely recognize her; there was no resemblance to the beautiful sister I knew. Her husband motioned me over to him, and in a low whisper, asked me not to show my surprise.

They had only planned on a short visit, but ended up staying for several weeks until my sister had recovered.

Worse than the physical pain she felt was the debilitating fear of another plane ride. But there was no other choice. It was the only means of returning home.

As we walked through the gate at the airport, she turned to me, "Please pray for me. I'm so scared. If I have to suffer as I did coming down, I swear to you, I will die."

"Don't be afraid, I promise you that you will not have to endure that agony on the way back," I assured her.

During the flurry of farewell hugs and kisses, I briefly excused myself on the pretext of checking the departure time again. I strolled to the monitor, and pretended to look for their flight information. I was in actuality, summoning my spirit guides and asking them to accompany my sister on her journey. I asked for them to do whatever was needed to keep her from suffering, and to stay by her side until she was safely back in her home.

Upon her return, my sister wrote, "Sis, if I have ever doubted you in the past, I never shall again. I still marvel at how my flight was so pleasant. Even as I arrived home, I felt comforted and safe."

Animal Guardians

Spirits can take forms other than human as you will see in the following story.

As a child I had a large "ghost dog" which stood by my bed every night. I knew he had to be a ghost dog because we were not allowed to have dogs in my family. Even if we had been allowed to have a dog, my mother would never have allowed the animal in the house. The dog looked like a Doberman Pinscher; black with eyes of fire, and he was as tall as the height of my bed.

I was both intrigued and frightened by my "ghost dog."

One night, feeling particularly bold, I decided to find out whether the dog was alive, or if it truly was a ghost. I crawled into bed and awaited his arrival. In a flash, he was there; big as life. Inch by inch, I reached my hand out from under the covers. Several times, I yanked it back until I could muster up more courage.

Finally, I did it. I pushed my hand toward the dog. My hand went right through him. I pulled it back and tried it again ... same thing. He just stood there. "He's a ghost." No doubt about it. I asked myself, "Why is he here?" Oh, how I wished I could tell someone. But I never did tell anyone about my guardian spirit dog; he remained my secret for a long, long time. I had learned that I would most likely be laughed at or disbelieved.

When I was younger, I had tried to share some of my psychic experiences and found to my surprise that everyone did not have invisible playmates, float on clouds and know when things were going to happen beforehand. I have read since, that psychic children may see ghost dogs or horses in the early stages of their childhood. In time, I forgot about the dog. I didn't tell Mother nor my sister and later, certainly, not my children. The episode was lost along with my other childhood adventures.

One day, many years later, after my own children were grown and raising families of their own, my daughter called to tell me of a psychic phenomenon, which saved her life.

She told me about a big black dog that looked like a Doberman Pinscher with eyes of fire, who jumped up on the hood of her car. She instinctively slammed on the brakes. As her car screeched to a stop, a large tractor-trailer rig roared by. She had stopped just in time to prevent a head-on collision with the truck.

"The dog vanished into thin air," she exclaimed. It was then, for the first time, I told her about my childhood "ghost dog." I was sure that my guardian dog and the dog who stopped her car were one and the same. I was grateful that he had protected her. I wonder how many times he protected not only me but also those I love.

In this chapter concerning different kinds of spirits, I would be remiss if I did not tell you of my most compelling spirits. They are not as widely known as some other types of spirits, like ghosts that haunt houses, guardian angels, and those which can take forms other than human, as mentioned in this chapter.

Spirit Masters

My most inspiring spirits consist of seven great sages, who lived through enough incarnations to purify their souls. They have by choice remained in spirit form to help deserving mankind. I have seen these great ones. The first time, I was in deep meditation. I opened my eyes to see all seven of them, looking down at me. I have called on them several times. Once when I had set a goal, which by human standards seemed impossible, I not only reached my goal but surpassed it.

I call these spirits the Secret Seven Mystic Circle (SSMC). I wonder why more people who are involved in the paranormal and metaphysical fields don't often make mention of them. I believe it is because one can only contact them through the doorway of the subconscious by way of the alpha brain wave frequency. They are of the higher realm. It takes years of study and meditation to reach them. Also, it seems that they only participate when the situation is far-reaching or one of global consequence.

The purpose for seeking their help must be beyond personal gain, such as a goal to help mankind, raising the vibrations of planet earth through artistic endeavor, feeding, housing and clothing the homeless, or inventions that raise the standards of our world. Upon discussing the SSMC with some very successful artists and inventors, I found that most of them admit to calling on a higher source. Two said that their spirit guides numbered seven. I wonder if it is the same group I am referring to or perhaps the spirits are attracted in accordance with the creative endeavor. An artist might attract great souls like Michelangelo and others from the same genre, while inventors might draw in Edison or Ford.

It is common knowledge that most of our great inventors and geniuses, consulted with spirits. Edison had regular round-table discussions with invisible forces, reserving a chair for each of them. He asked questions and received answers; taking notes during each session.

Throughout history, many famous artists, inventors, and scientists admitted to receiving assistance that was outside the realm of human intervention. Ford, and Einstein among them.

The path of the subconscious is a mysterious journey. A creative genius can paint or sculpt a masterpiece, but if you would ask him to sit down and create the exact same piece, he cannot because it came from the subconscious mind.

Greatness is probably always achieved through the alpha brain wave frequency, the path to the divine; the world of invisible creativity.

Earthbound Spirits

I learned about earthbound spirits firsthand by living for several years in a haunted house. Earthbound spirits are confused discarnate entities—those people who, after their death, remain attached to the material plane in a lower astral body instead of going on. Some earthbound spirits are held by an emotional tie from their recent life that they do not understand, or by strong earthly desires they are unable to break. Others are held by a belief that they are not dead because they never believed in an afterlife or had never thought about anything more than the temporal existence. They do not realize they are dead, and they attempt to continue their ordinary lives, unaware that they cannot be seen. Many times, spirits are held to the earth plane by family or friends whose ceaseless mourning will not release the spirit to move on.

I must tell you about my own conflicts with earthbound spirits who did not know they were dead. The following story is a real-life experience.

Shortly after moving into my new home, I awakened one night, certain that someone was staring at me. The dim light that filtered through the window revealed a hooded figure standing beside my bed. As I frantically switched on the light, the apparition vanished. I sat straight up in bed. Was someone playing a gruesome prank? During the weeks that followed, many more strange events ensued. I began to realize that my 100-year-old house must be haunted. Trying not to believe it, I told myself that my imagination was playing tricks on me. But I knew I was not imagining the cold chills which encircled me every time I got up in the middle of the night. I would hear shuffling of feet, rustling of heavy fabric and the sound of someone on the stairs, constantly coming or going.

My old house had a large eat-in kitchen but at times it felt very crowded even when only two people were at the table. Things would fall to the floor as if someone had bumped them. It felt like the room was full of people, making it awkward to prepare a meal.

Everyone who visited me knew there was something very strange about my house. Ellen, my niece, came running downstairs after staying the night, shouting, "Auntie, do you know there are strange people upstairs?"

One friend refused to come again after only one visit. He said that from the moment he entered my house, something pressed so heavily on his chest that he could hardly breathe. He did not have this problem anywhere else.

My fiancee felt their presence so clearly that he would automatically say "excuse me" when passing in front of one of them. Then he would feel embarrassed when he realized there was no one there.

One of them materialized on two different occasions. He appeared to be about forty, medium build, muscular with straight dark hair. He was dressed in blue jeans and a white sport shirt.

My brother lived with me at that time. One evening I was returning from church when I thought I saw my brother standing in the doorway leading into the living room. His hand was pressed against the back of his head, as if in deep thought, and his back was toward the front door. The light was on and I could see clearly through the glass door.

I tapped on the door but he paid no attention. I knocked louder and shouted, "Jim, let me in." Still he made no move toward the door. I fished in my purse for my keys and let myself in. I walked toward him, wondering why he had not responded. There, right before my eyes, the figure vanished. I ran upstairs and found my brother sound asleep. I had to face it ... it was a ghost.

On another occasion, my friend, Edith, came to me for

consolation. Her husband, Hank, had died. His funeral was to be that evening and she was finding it hard to deal with.

As we sat, talking about him, Hank walked right past us, swinging his arms as was his custom. He was wearing the same white shirt and dark trousers as usual. Edith nearly fainted as he disappeared into the foyer.

The next day, my brother Jim and I were sitting in the living room discussing the phenomena concerning our invisible inhabitants. These spirits had done many strange things, and I began to realize they must have powers beyond anything I could ever imagine. We never knew what to expect next.

Suddenly, Jim gasped and pointed toward the staircase. We stared in amazement as a grey cloud descended down the stairs. At first, the cloud was indistinct but as it floated downward, it began to take the shape of a man. We sat speechless as it drifted into my bedroom, which was located next to where we were seated.

We could not see around the doorway, so we got up and peeked inside to see what bizarre happening this could be. The mysterious cloud formation had landed on my bed. A closer observation revealed Dan, my renter from upstairs. He seemed to be in a deep sleep. Then, to our astonishment, in a grey cloud, his shoes materialized beside the bed.

I had previously noticed how the spirits disliked visitors in the house, but I could never have anticipated such a show of defiance. It seemed that somehow, they put Dan into a deep somnambulist trance and literally teleported him down the stairs into my bedroom.

Dan left the next day without a word as to what he had experienced. Perhaps he did not know how he got downstairs. But, like many of my visitors, he wanted no part of it.

I had always felt that the spirits were people who had lived in my house and loved the place. I didn't think of them as sinister or threatening. However, this last incident, as well as some that followed, could possibly change my mind. With so many peculiar things happening in succession, I began to wonder if I should consider ridding my house of these bizarre characters.

Should I have my house exorcised, as had been suggested to me repeatedly by friends who had experienced this phenomenon? Did I have the right? They were there before I bought the house. What if I was the intruder? These thoughts meandered through my mind as I considered the money I had spent, buying and renovating my house.

I also remembered the experiences I had endured, trying to learn how to live with these ghosts. My mind wandered back to my efforts to conquer my fear and to how difficult it had been just acknowledging their presence.

I remembered the time I turned out all the lights and walked through my huge house, scared to death ... surrounded by an unearthly chill. I wanted desperately to reach for the light switch. I knew that if I did, I would probably never have enough courage to be alone in the dark again. I had to stand my ground. I reasoned that if I acknowledged their right to live there, perhaps they would reciprocate. They seemed to know what I was thinking, for the chills suddenly ceased.

"Aha," I thought, "They are using mental telepathy." Knowing their secret, I could learn to communicate with them.

With experimentation, I found that if I wanted an answer to something, I'd ask them telepathically. If the answer was "no" they would surround me with chills. If the answer was "yes" the room had a warm atmosphere.

If I said, when leaving, "I'll be back soon" or some such message, the room remained pleasant. But if I forgot to greet them when returning, they surrounded me with chills. I soon learned that they liked to be acknowledged. Apparently, I was the only one who had ever made an effort to know them. I was their only friend.

My fiancee had never encountered invisible people, so he had to learn to say "hello" and "good-bye" to them the same as I. It took a while for him to reconcile himself to them. The minute he stepped into the room, they would surround him with chills, follow him around, making noises and just generally seeing to it that he was most uncomfortable.

He finally decided that he must have it out with them. He went upstairs, knowing they would follow. Seating himself in a chair and as if talking to a brother, he said, "See here. I have accepted you. Why won't you let me be your friend, too? It seems that your only friend is my fiancee. It seems to me that you could use another. How about it?"

They accepted him, even to the point of following him home to his apartment, one night.

He said that as he arrived at his condo, they surrounded him with chills. We believe that they were trying to tell him that they didn't want him to leave.

He told me that he went to the door and opened it, saying, "You don't belong here. You had better go back to the house." As they left, he felt one of them pat him on the back.

It was after our marriage that we found some other peculiarities concerning them. It seems to take a lot of energy for them to materialize. We found that they can tap into and use the power from a thunder storm, especially if there is a lot of lightning. They also use the energy generated from human behavior such as sexual encounters.

The first time we noticed this, was during a thunder storm. We were making love when the lightning flashed. There by our bed stood a small elderly gentleman. He was bald except for a little fringe around the edge. He wore rimless glasses, dropped down on his nose and was dressed in a blue chambray shirt and overalls.

I finally discussed these entities with a Spiritualist minister. She suggested that I let these spirits know that they were dead. So the next time I sensed their presence, I asked them, "Do you people know you are dead?"

The room suddenly became very chilly, and the atmosphere was one of shocked silence. They were stunned. I realized I had been far too blunt. I tried to smooth it over by telling them about my own dying experience, of the euphoria and how much they were missing by staying here on earth.

I said, "It can't be so terrible. You're dead and you don't even know it." I explained that there is no death as we know it, but rather a new dimension far more splendid than anything the earth has to offer. They seemed to understand but I was totally unprepared for their reaction to the thought of leaving me, their only friend.

During the afternoon, my husband and I decided to take a nap. We went upstairs to the back bedroom. Louis fell sound asleep but I had much on my mind. I lay there thinking about all the strange things my invisible friends seemed capable of doing.

I sensed their presence, the chill that told me they were near. They seemed to know that I had mastered astral projection for they asked me to join them in spirit. Wanting to make up for my earlier brashness, I agreed.

I had no sooner left my body than they told me to look

back at my pillow. There, on our pillows, lay two grotesque-looking skulls. I realized it was a trick as one of them said, "Surely, you don't want to return to that."

I knew they valued me as a friend but I had no idea to what lengths they would go to keep me with them. I scampered back into my body.

They had not given up yet. That night, I went to bed early while Louis stayed downstairs to watch TV. As I began to drift off, I became aware of a hooded figure bending over me. In an instant, another similar figure appeared on the other side of my bed.

I thought I was having a nightmare until I felt the sheet being drawn across my chest, pinning my arms at my side.

Tighter and tighter, they pulled the sheet. I couldn't breathe. I struggled but to no avail. Then I knew ... these spirits planned to take me with them. After what seemed like an eternity, finally, I was able to scream, "No. No. This is wrong."

My screams must have startled them for they let me go. Then I realized how difficult it was for them to leave me, their friend, the only one who had ever tried to communicate with them.

I explained to them (via telepathy as always) that only God can decide when our period on earth is over. That it was obviously their time but not mine. I assured them that I would join them when my time was up.

After their departure, the house became peaceful and quiet. Everyone noticed the change immediately and our friends began to visit again.

One evening as we sat watching TV, I sensed that a spirit was in the room. Without thinking I exclaimed, "Oh, please don't come back."

I was immediately sorry for my outburst. I wanted to apologize but it was too late. The spirit had vanished. I prayed for this lost one. Being earthbound, they probably need guidance and counsel until they are safely on the other side. I could have been a steadying influence if I had not been so selfish.

I think of the people in England who boast of their ghosts. I wonder if the earth bound spirits shouldn't be told that they're dead. At least they could then, have a choice of leaving or staying.

In summary, let me say that I have had many encounters with lots of different kinds of spirits and I have never had a really bad experience with them. They are just people like you and I who no longer have a physical body. Sometimes they need guidance, much like you and I, especially if they are earthbound.

If you should sense that a spirit is nearby, envision a pure white light surrounding and protecting you then say, "If you are of the Divine force, you may stay. If not, I command you to leave."

You can attract a spirit or spirits through a Ouija board, automatic writing or through a medium, or while endeavoring to accomplish some psychic venture such as astral travel, or perhaps through no fault of your own, as in the case of my haunted house.

It is important to keep your thoughts on a higher plane so as not to attract the wrong type of spirits. The black spirits dwell on lower planes and you will not attract them if your thoughts are pure. Before delving into any of the psychic sciences, channel your thoughts to the higher realms. Dwell on the Divine Presence, where nothing but good can befall you.

Technique For Spiritual Protection

Do this exercise every morning to help prevent accidents during the day, deter negative thoughts from cluttering your mind, and to repel psychic attacks from any source. You may use this technique to protect not only yourself, but your possessions, house and loved ones.

1. Visualize a clear, colorless light ... a pure light ... coming down and entering your crown chakra.

2. Visualize this bright white light spreading throughout your entire body and surrounding it.

3. Repeat positive, loving mental affirmations.

Technique To Contact Spirit Guides

1. In a quiet room, relax your physical body and conscious self, and allow your mind to release its cares.

2. Light a white candle; this will be your focal point. If it helps you relax, play some soothing background music.

3. Gaze steadily at the candle; see your spirit guide enter the area where you are.

4. Mentally ask your guide whatever questions or information you desire.

5. If you wish, you may use automatic writing at this time, as long as it does not disturb the flow of communication from your guide.

6. When you are finished, thank your guide for being in your life and bid the spirit farewell.

. . . .

CHAPTER THREE

Subconscious Mind: Your Obedient Servant

Can you imagine having a genie who carries out your every command and never sleeps nor questions your judgment? You have such a genie—your subconscious mind. This part of your mind is 90 to 95 percent more powerful than your conscious, waking mind.

Your subconscious mind thinks only in pictures; never in words or abstract concepts. As an example, if I ask you to think of a house, you will not think of the letters h-o-u-s-e. You will instead see the image of an actual specific house as a mental picture. This is the way your subconscious sees every thought.

Never go to sleep to forget an unpleasant experience. It is at this time, while drowsy or asleep that the subconscious is most active. During sleep your brain waves change frequencies from beta state—conscious, to alpha and theta states—subconscious. Your subconscious works with the picture in your mind. Since it never questions your judgment, it assumes that the picture in your mind is what you want to accomplish.

As an example, let's say you had a fight with your spouse and go to sleep to forget it. What picture is in your mind? The fight; right? This genie can work only from pictures. So, it sets about to see that you have more fights. Since it never sleeps, it will materialize that picture.

The most important thing you can ever learn about this genie is; it does not know the difference between a real and an imaginary experience. If you (think of) give him a picture of a happy event, instead of the fight which you are trying to forget, he will believe that picture and materialize it.

Remember, we are talking about that powerful genie, your subconscious mind. Your conscious mind rules your senses—smelling, tasting, hearing, seeing and touching. It reasons and questions your every move. It can be a trouble-maker at times. It takes into account the many negatives with which you have been plagued since birth. Did you know that by the time you entered school, you had heard the word "no" 60,000 times? You also heard such negative phrases as "You can't do that," "You'll never amount to anything," and "You'll catch your death of cold!"

You carry these negatives with you, so when your sub-conscious mind (your genie) is trying to respond to your command, your conscious mind is saying, "You can't do it. It is not reasonable and logical!"

Since your subconscious works best in your alpha/theta brain wave frequency (when you are totally relaxed), you can see how important it is to give it a pleasant picture before going to sleep. When you are drowsy or asleep, your senses are dulled. You don't see, hear, smell, taste or feel in a normal fashion during this time, because the conscious mind is dormant.

Your conscious mind is governed by the beta brain wave frequency. This is the every day state of consciousness. Your conscious mind goes to sleep but your subconscious *never* does. So it is imperative that you give this genie something positive to work on.

Your subconscious is governed by the alpha/theta brainwave frequency, the state achieved while completely relaxed or drowsy. This is when this genie works best, while the conscious mind is inactive and out of the way.

Though the alpha/theta state is automatic when you are in deep relaxation or falling asleep, it can be deliberately induced at any time. Use the following technique: Sit or lie in a comfortable position in a quiet place. Feel yourself relaxing more and more with each breath. As you inhale, let go of all cares and problems. Paint a picture of what you would most like to achieve. See the picture as if it has already been accomplished. Accept this picture totally, with feeling, as you relax.

As you slip into quiet relaxation, your genie is already working on materializing your picture and will continue to do so as long as you remain in this relaxed state. You may wonder how you will know if you are in your alpha state. If you are reasoning or questioning whether it can happen, you have slipped back into your beta brain wave frequency which is controlled by the reasoning, logical conscious mind.

Your genie,—your subconscious—does not question or reason. It cannot make a decision of its own, but takes data exactly as given to it from your conscious mind. It trusts the picture you give it, even when it is an imaginary one. Remember, *the subconscious does not know the difference between a real and an imaginary experience.* I repeat this because it is of monumental importance.

If you slip, don't give up. Go back to the technique. Start over. The rewards far outweigh the effort.

Your picture should be as complete as you can make it. The reason some people might fail in this technique is because they either don't know what they want or the picture is too vague. It will work every time *if* you follow the instructions completely. The picture must include every detail. It is like trying to order something from a catalog. You must know the color, size and style to get results.

Unfortunately, your genie can work against you if you give him a negative picture. He is impersonal—he doesn't care what kind of picture you give him. It is his position to materialize the picture, good or bad. If you see riches, he'll give you riches and if you see poverty, he'll see that you get it. Indeed, what you see is what you get. The images you feed your subconscious mind are creating your world. Beliefs are thoughts, thoughts are pictures, words and thoughts are things—they materialize.

Our greatest failures as well as our grandest triumphs were merely pictures in our minds at first. Nothing can happen until someone thinks of it. It is much like incubation. Many things that have transpired in our lives come from seeds that were planted in our childhood.

When I was a youngster, I lived alongside the Ohio river. I saw steamboats in lighted splendor passing down the river every night. The people on board looked so grand as they dined and danced. I thought, "Some day, I will dance the night away on board such a fine vessel." The seeds were planted. As an adult, I have enjoyed many luxury cruises ... the seeds bearing fruit.

The universal law of consequence says that one has the

free will to think, say or do whatever one wants to do at all times. However, one is personally responsible for the outcome of these choices, and must handle the consequences. In other words, "What you sow, so shall you reap." This law works unerringly. You may choose whether to make it work for or against you. Ignorance of this law does not negate the consequences.

You might say, "It is not fair. I did not know this when I formed the thought!" Your subconscious might answer, "I'm not responsible. I did my job. I materialized the picture you gave me!"

Fake it 'till you make it!' Act as though the thing desired exists before you lay hold of it. This genie doesn't know the difference between a real and an imaginary picture! This statement is the key, it works every time! *Your subconscious does not know the difference between a real and an imaginary image.*

When Napoleon decided to become the emperor of France, everyone laughed, "Who ever heard of a five-foot emperor?" But Napoleon was aware of the power of his subconscious genie, and he knew that he could make this genie think he was already the emperor, and it would materialize the picture. He hired an actor to teach him how to dress, walk, talk and sit like an emperor. He asked himself, "What would an emperor talk about? What kind of pictures does he put in his mind?" Even, " How would he mount a horse?"

He saw himself as emperor every waking moment, and dreamed of it at night. His subconscious, like an obedient servant, materialized the picture. By the time the picture was complete in Napoleon's mind, he was indeed Emperor of France!

Beginner's luck is a perfect example. Someone is teaching

you a game. They tell you all the objectives; what you are supposed to do. You have the complete picture of how to win this game. But how did you win against someone who has played it for many years?

You had only one picture; that of winning! Remember what happened after playing with people who have lost? You saw the picture of how to lose and your beginner's luck changed; because your picture changed. Look at the youngster who plays baseball and has struck out many times. He steps up to the plate and what does he see? He sees his failures and strikes out again.

Our minds are like a movie projector. It can only project the picture that you load into the projector. If you want a different picture, you must change the film. Earl Nightingale says, "You cannot sow corn and reap wheat, no more than you can sit in front of the stove and expect heat until you put in the fuel."

Have you ever, as a child, participated in a cruel game of telling a well person how bad he looks? With persistence, even a healthy child will become ill. He begins to see the picture the gang is projecting.

Claude Bristol's book, "As A Man Thinketh" is an excellent treatise on how to change your life by the way you think. Nightingale's "Strangest Secret" tells us that we are what we think about. And the Bible says, "Be careful what you set your heart upon, for you shall surely have it."

Listening to subliminal tapes is one of the best ways to connect with the subconscious mind. The message is embedded in the sound of ocean waves or music. Through this 21st century technology, you can change your life by reprogramming the way you think!

Your conscious mind hears only the music or the waves,

but the subconscious mind hears the message which is emanating too low for conscious perception. Both the conscious and subconscious mind are being programed with no obvious effort.

While you go about your normal day, listening to soothing waves or music, your genie forms pictures from messages such as, "I am a success. I respect myself. I deserve the best."

It is phenomenal, all the things the subconscious mind does without our conscious awareness. Like a computer, around the clock, it runs all the body systems. It receives 100,000,000 impulses and signals per second from our body and senses, and yet, we use less than ten percent of our brain. Subliminal tapes help us to rid our lives of the negative programming which we have been harboring in our brain all our lives.

It is now believed that we learn while still in the womb. Like a sponge, we absorb information, much of it negative. Expectant mothers are being taught to be mindful of their moods, attitudes and even their thoughts. What an awesome responsibility awaits a woman who hopes to become a mother! But imagine the tremendous boon to mankind as mothers and doctors become more in tune with positive prenatal programming. Imagine the beautiful, collective mind consciousness that will come from these children who have been influenced while in the womb by loving, positive, happy mothers.

Once, two ladies approached me in a park. They sat down on the bench next to me and we struck up a conversation. One of the ladies seemed to be in great pain. I asked them if they had ever tried visualization. They said that they had.

"Visualization is really faith, you know," I said.

In surprise, the woman said, "No, I didn't know. How is it faith?"

"Faith is: believing so intently, that you can actually see the completed picture. If it is a healing you desire, you must, in your mind's eye, see yourself free of the affliction or have someone else see it for you. Someone must see, without a doubt, your freedom from the disease. It's healing through visualization."

A modern conception of this could be visualizing a computer with a tracer beam which could scan the body and discover those areas which need healing. Then with your mind, you would send a laser through the body to erase these diseased areas. You would then press the "erase" button to clear the system.

Since nature abhors a vacuum, you must replace anything that was removed, so you would replace the disease with a white light. You would send the white light into the body, filling it from head to toe to prevent the disease from returning.

Visualization is most affective when your conscious waking mind is at rest or dormant. Meditation and relaxation exercises will bring you into the alpha/theta brain wave frequencies perfect for this powerful visualization.

Another way to induce the alpha/theta brain frequency and unleash the power of your personal genie is through the exciting imaging of cyber-optics. At first glance these images appear to be mazes of lines and color with no apparent order or clearly defined picture. Upon further study incredible three dimensional images pop out at the viewer. Where once there was a confused pattern of lines, suddenly a clear precise image appears ... as if from nowhere.

The first time I experienced cyber-optics was truly incredible. I had learned about brain-wave frequency and neuron function through my education in psychology and metaphysics, so I knew what was happening as I viewed this unfamiliar maze-like poster.

I was in a metaphysical bookstore when my interest was drawn to a group of very excited people in the back of the store. I was surprised to find that everyone's attention was focused on a large poster hanging on the wall.

"This is terrific!" I said. "This poster quickly puts one into a theta brain-wave frequency. Usually it takes a lot of time and meditation to achieve that."

A voice behind me asked, "How would you know that?"

"I'm a doctor of metaphysics. You can see the effect it has on these people. Just look at them."

The man glanced over to see each customer take their turn gazing into the poster. It wasn't hard to notice that when a person stood still and stared into the dot matrix design, their breathing changed and their eyes began to shine as if they were in a deep and relaxed state. The perfect state for visualization.

"I must have this poster!" I said, "I don't even care what the price is!"

Don Tolman is the developer of cyber-optic posters and has allowed me to use this wonderful phenomenon. We call the magic of the cyber-optic world *third eye* viewing because it induces and strengthens different levels of consciousness.

As you study these cyber-optic posters, sometimes referred to as *thetagraphs*, you are strengthening and increasing the size of the neurons in your brain. These posters are actually neuro-optic enhancement instruments. They can facilitate change in your brain wave frequency and stimulate endorphins; giving you a real sense of well being.

Researchers now believe that changes in brain wave frequencies can also help cure depression and other emotional disorders. People who generally seem happy and have the ability to always see the bright side, may have different brain wave patterns than people who are pessimistic and depressed. By tapping into your alpha/theta levels you may be reshaping your daily outlook from one of stress or fear into calm self-assurance. It is true that people who meditate on a daily basis often seem happier and have less stress in their lives. I have seen very positive results using cyber-optics, even in the most extreme cases.

A 40-year-old woman with the mind of a child was continually frightened and upset. She was visited with horrible episodes of shaking and depression and suffered from severe anxiety. With her limited verbal skills, straight forward approaches were not helping.

I placed a *third eye* poster across her lap and asked her to tell me what she saw.

"Oh, it's magic! There are stars, mountains, hearts and swirls."

She made swirling motions with her fingers and pointed at each magic image in the poster. She began to relax and grow calm. Her shaking stopped. Then she looked up at me and yawned! " I feel so good," she said. "I think I'll take a nap." She went directly into the alpha/theta frequency.

I have since shared this magic with many people. These posters can be used to induce a "hypnogogic" state. Once there, you can visualize your goals as if you have already achieved them. You can also overcome stress and boost your brain power. Try the cyber-optic poster on page 57.

Here is the technique for using these posters. Bifocals or trifocals will slow your progress, so I suggest that you purchase an inexpensive pair of magnifying eye glasses just for viewing the poster.

The technique: Hold the poster almost against your nose. Stare into a dark spot and allow your eyes to defocus. Keep staring for a few seconds. Move the poster back away from your face very slowly to a comfortable viewing position. Once the magic image appears continue to stare at the poster without losing the picture for five to ten minutes.

During this time the magic image will seem to stand in midair or it will recede away from you. If the picture comes forward you are viewing it convergently (in alpha 3D) but if the picture recedes you are into divergent viewing via the theta brain wave frequency. Either way is good but you want to keep working with it until you can view it divergently because this method takes you straight into "Thetaland". This is the ultimate for visualization.

Whether achieving your alpha/theta state of consciousness via relaxation, meditation or by focussing on a cyber-optic image, the objective is to alter your state of consciousness to where visualization can be enhanced. Visualization is the key to unlocking your all powerful genie.

Technique to Induce the Alpha State of Consciousness for Achieving Your Goals

The best time to do this exercise is just before going to sleep and when first awakening.

1. Sit or lie in a comfortable position in a quiet atmosphere.

2. Focus on your breathing. Relax more and more with each breath.

3. As you exhale, let go of all your cares and problems.

4. Paint a complete picture in your mind of the situation you wish to bring about. See only that picture. See it as already yours.

5. Accept it and give thanks.

Technique For Cyber-Optic Or Third Eye Viewing:

1. Hold the poster against your nose.

2. Stare into a dark spot and let your eyes defocus.

3. Move the poster away from you until you reach a comfortable viewing position.

4. Continue to stare at the poster until the image appears.

5. Continue to stare at the poster without losing the picture until you can see the image divergently—receding away from you, as well as convergently—toward you as if in midair.

6. Once in "Thetaland" visualize what you want as if it has already been achieved.

CHAPTER FOUR

. . . .

Astral Projection

The term "astral projection" means the ability to send the spirit form, called the astral or etheric body, out of the physical body. This is also known as an *out-of-body* experience or *leaving the body*. The astral or etheric body is the exact duplicate of the physical body. It carries with it our consciousness and our thoughts. When one has an out-of-body experience, the physical body is passive, as if asleep, while the astral body is aware of what goes on but from an entirely different viewpoint than that of the physical body.

The real self is spirit. The body is the house the spirit occupies. The spirit or astral body weighs about one and one half ounces. This was determined by scientific tests which measured the weight of the physical body alive, and as recorded at the exact moment of death. The astral body is connected to the physical body by a silver cord which is the umbilical link between the two bodies. Hundreds of people who have experienced astral travel speak of this silver cord which never diminishes in diameter no matter how far one travels.

Over the years, scientific studies have shown that astral projection is a naturally occurring, widespread human phenomenon. It happens spontaneously more often than you may realize. The astral body frequently leaves the physical body during sleep. This is what happens when you wake with a start as if you're falling. You have been in the astral while asleep. Many scientists believe we leave the body while sleeping. This gives the body time to rest. The astral body may leave the physical body when one is unconscious or anesthetized. Many people experience astral projection for the first time during surgery, or a trauma so intense that their astral body is driven from the physical. In these cases, astral projection takes place without conscious effort.

In *Memories, Dreams, Reflections* Carl Jung writes, "I would never have imagined that any such experience was possible. It was not a product of imagination. The visions and experiences were utterly real; there was nothing subjective about them; they all had a quality of absolute objectivity."

You don't have to be particularly psychic to learn to induce astral projection at will; some of our finest universities offer classes and instruction on astral projection. It is wise to learn the proper technique so that you control the experience; then you can benefit from the special powers of the astral body.

There is a scientifically demonstrated link between theta brain waves and out-of-body experiences. Theta waves come between alpha level (8 to 12 cycles) which occurs during relaxation and delta (4-7 cycles), which occur during deep sleep. Theta waves generally manifest when a person is involved in a deep, altered-state-of-consciousness, such as achieved while meditating or creating intense mental imagery. You can learn to generate theta waves through biofeedback or by viewing a cyber-optic poster, or using special syn-chronizing brain wave tapes.

Astral projection demonstrates to me that the mind is an entity in its own right, something distinct from the brain and body. Once you find yourself outside the physical body, you will realize that the body is not the real you. You are spirit, the image and likeness of God. Once you have mastered astral projection, you will never again fear death. The body, in actuality, is a prison. People who have had out-of-body experiences are no longer materialists; they have had a literal demonstration of personal immortality.

I myself had a death experience and it was the most euphoric experience of my life! There are no words that can begin to express the feeling of freedom and ecstasy! I have also experienced astral projection, which is much the same except, dying is much more euphoric.

One lady was cured of her poor self-image by astral projection. When she looked back at her body, she liked what she saw. She had never before thought of herself as being attractive.

A man I know is so accustomed to going in and out of his body that sometimes, he doesn't know which body he is occupying until he attempts to pick up the coffee pot. At such times, he mutters, "I'll have to go back to the bedroom and get that darn equipment!"

One man claims to have rendezvous with friends and associates on the astral plane. They can project at will. Distance makes no difference. They live miles apart and meet this way on a regular basis. He says, "It sure beats driving." He suggests that if you have an especially vivid dream where another person is involved, call that other person and see if he or she has had the same dream. You may find that you are meeting in the astral.

One lady practiced by sending her thoughts to another part of the house. After a little practice, she began finding herself in the room she was thinking of. When she would go back to the bedroom she would find her body still in the bed.

The first step is to know you can do it. The technique is not complicated but will require some practice. Any thought of being afraid or doubting your ability will prove detrimental. Try to acquire the attitude, "If others can do it, I can do it." One should never use astral projection for a negative purpose, such as spying on someone. Negativity can jerk you out of the astral and back into your body, and it can be a nasty shock.

The technique: Plan your attempt at astral travel carefully. Your demeanor should be tranquil but with a spirit of anticipation, as if planning any other journey. Nighttime is best. Go quietly to your bedroom. Wear loose clothing. Make the room a comfortable temperature. Draw the shade to close out as much light as possible. Sit or lie in a comfortable position and relax as much as possible.

Take a few deep breaths, relaxing more and more with each breath. Keep your eyes closed and visualize a flame. Keep staring at the flame. Bring it close to you. Become one with the flame.

Notice that you are becoming increasingly heavy all over. This is the hypnogogic state, that trancelike state you pass through while going to sleep or while awakening. Your head is weighty on the pillow. Your eyes are heavy. You want to go to sleep but you must not allow sleep, yet. This drowsy state is most important!

You feel a deep heaviness all over. Your head sags. Your breathing becomes deeper and deeper. A vague dreaminess sweeps over you. Everything is far, far away. All tension is gone. You have blocked everything from your mind but astral travel.

Say these words three times, "I am traveling in the astral but I am remaining aware of all that I see and do. I shall recall everything when I am back in my physical body."

Lie comfortably relaxed. Will your astral body to leave your physical body. Feel as though you are forcing another body out of yourself.

Feel it withdrawing from the flesh body. You feel like a cork rising out of water. You become aware of a tingling sensation.

There comes a moment when the tingling almost ceases and a sudden coolness comes over you as though something has left you. This is a crucial moment. Don't move. This only signals that you are succeeding.

Suddenly you feel a slight electric shock! The pattern of your breathing changes. You find yourself looking down at your physical body, wondering what to do next.

Let yourself float like a soap bubble on the air currents. Keep your eyes closed and allow yourself to rise. Feel yourself floating upward like a puff ball on a summer breeze. You are light as a feather.

Look back at your body, lying motionless as you float about like Peter Pan. Now, you know that this is the real you. You have taken your senses with you. Notice that your flesh body does not move. It does not see, but you see with your eyes closed. Note the vivid colors. You can sink your hand through a wall with no sensation. How easily you move! You travel on the speed of thought. Keep your thoughts within your room, for now.

Notice the silver cord that connects the two bodies. As

you move away, the silver cord stretches without diminishing in diameter.

Now, let your astral body drift down to the floor. Take another look at your physical body. You will remember everything that has happened. Now it is time to return to your body. Do so and sleep peacefully. Once you have mastered this technique, you can travel astrally any time you desire.

It is best to stay within your own bedroom for the first few flights. Remember, you travel on thought waves, so be careful what you think of when in the astral.

As an example of why this is important; you could think of an ocean and suddenly find yourself there, flying just above the water. If you became scared, your thoughts would send you suddenly back into your body with a shock! Any negative thought such as fear will result in being immediately jerked back into your body. So, until you become comfortable while astral traveling, plan beforehand what you will think about. I knew of one man who forgot to guard his thoughts and suddenly felt himself shooting toward the sun. The fright, of course, sent him plummeting back into his body.

This technique may seem prolonged but it is well worth the persistence required. Read over the instructions several times before trying it. Imagine that you are in actual practice so you will be able to go through the exercise without looking at notes.

You might practice sending your thoughts to another part of the house as did the lady I referred to earlier. There are many techniques. This is one I have found to be most effective.

We travel places in our mental body and think nothing of it. Astral travel is the same. Try this practice: Let your mind wander to a scene on the beach; a vacation, perhaps. All at once you are there, looking at the water, the surfers, the sun bathers; people walking hand in hand on the sand.

Notice that during this scene, you were no longer in your living room, because you can only think of one thing or experience one thing at a time. You were on the beach. You just took a trip in your mental body! It is called "thought."

The difference when traveling in the astral body is that you take your senses and consciousness with you. Your physical body stays at home, motionless, because your astral body now possesses your senses. Astral projection is as easy as mental projection. We erect barriers because it is unfamiliar to us.

After a little practice, it rather sneaks up on you. It might happen something like this: You think of a place and plan to deliberately be there in your mental body (that is, to think about this place; possibly the beach). Suddenly, you notice something is different! You feel the sand under your feet. You actually see people and places. You feel the wind in your face. You smell the salt air. You taste the salt water on your tongue. Your senses are alive!

When you are just thinking about a place, you do not take your senses with you. Only your astral body has this ability. You are astral traveling! See how easy it is?

The phenomenon of bi-location is similar to astral projection except the body may show up in two different places.

The etheric (astral) body is an exact replica of the physical body but it has a finer vibrational quality. It contains all the sensory equipment as well as the consciousness, which is why the projection of the etheric body can be seen and heard; it can be recognized and identified by other people. Many cases of bi-location have been documented. In his book "Wisdom of the Mystic Masters," Joseph Weed recounts the case of Monsignor Alphonsus, the abbot of Arienzo in Italy.

While in a deep sleep at the monastery, the monsignor

was also in Rome, leading prayer services for the dying Pope. This was authenticated by the Dominican Observatory and Augustinian Orders along with those in attendance.

Another notable case concerns the multi-appearances of the great Tibetan mystic and saint, Milarepa. Near the hour of his death, he was seen in his physical body in Asia, Tibet, Afghanistan, India, Ceylon and the Malay states. His followers in each of these places actually touched him.

Several times, I have experienced this phenomenon. My daughter who lives in another state, tells me that I am often with her at her house, when I am actually in my own home in Florida. "How clearly do you see me? Do I talk to you? Is it usually at night?" I asked her, for I am not aware of this.

"Most often you are in my kitchen, watching me as I prepare the evening meal. You never say anything. You seem to be just observing what I am doing," she answered.

"Does my sudden appearance frighten you? Is it like seeing a ghost?" I asked.

"No, you don't look like a ghost. I see you just the way you always look; no difference. I love having you with me even if you don't carry on a conversation," she assured me.

Another bi-location experience concerned my church. I usually attend yoga classes there on Thursday evenings. I reported to Martha, our yoga instructor, "I will be absent from class for at least six weeks. I am going to be taking classes in parapsychology at the university."

After a few weeks absence from yoga class, Martha came into the library where I was selecting a text book for class. "Do you know that you are still in yoga class every Thursday evening?"

"No, Martha, I am in parapsychology class at the university on Thursday evenings."

"I know that. The first time we saw you in yoga class, I immediately called the university. They assured me that you were also in parapsychology class."

I asked, "How clearly do you see me? Is there anything different about me?"

"No. You look just like you do right now. There are five of us students who can see you in class," she told me.

The following is an example of astral projection, but could be termed bi-location.

A man of Indian extraction stopped at my door and asked whether I rented rooms. My home is a large two-story house. My brother lived with me but I had not thought of renting rooms. Something prompted me to ask him in. He followed me into the kitchen. I made him a cup of coffee which he never touched nor did he mention renting a room.

Instead he proceeded to tell me everything about my life from the day I was born to the present time; things that no one knew except God and me. I sat there, dumbfounded!

Finally, after arousing myself from the initial shock, I asked, "How can you possibly know all this? I have never seen you before."

"I have loved you always. I have been with you since time began," he answered calmly, after which, he walked straight into the living room and sat down on the couch beside my brother.

I was stunned; bewildered, wondering how this man, whom I had never seen, could know my life history. What did he mean by, "I have been with you since time began?" In utter astonishment, I began to wonder if the Divine, Himself, was speaking to me. But how?

Finally, I could stand the suspense no longer. I walked into the living room. "How can you have so much knowledge about my life? How can you know personal details about things I have never told anyone? Why are you aware of the corporation that I formed. You have just revealed knowledge of everything that has ever happened in my life! No one knows most of these things but God and me!"

"I don't know what you are talking about. I wasn't here," he protested.

"My brother was sitting here all the time. He can attest to the fact that you have been here in my kitchen for almost an hour, talking your head off! You cannot deny it!"

He stopped for a moment and thought. Then he asked, "Are you familiar with astral projection?"

"Yes, we are studying astral projection at the university, in parapsychology class. It's referred to as etheric projection sometimes. This phenomenon happens when the spirit leaves the body and goes to other places," I answered.

"In India we accept astral projection as a natural occurrence. We go in and out of our bodies as children and continue all our lives. So you see; my body was in your kitchen but I was not. I have no idea who spoke to you while I was away."

"Has this ever happened to you before; an entity speaking through you?" I asked.

"Probably many times but only once that I am aware of. When I was studying in Tibet, an entity spoke through me and told a Llama such great truths, that even today he cannot reveal them all, but I have no idea what was said."

Martha could not have known anything of this latest incident. But upon our next encounter she exclaimed, "You are still in yoga class but who is that Indian with you?"

I experienced my next bi-location while my husband and I were vacationing in Mexico. He awakened to see me sitting on the edge of my bed, brushing my hair. What astounded him was that I was also sound asleep in my bed.

He explained, "I looked from one figure to the other and could not distinguish which one was the real you."

I have frequently wondered if, in cases of UFO abductions, it might be the etheric body that is abducted, rather than the dense physical body. Since it carries with it all the sensory equipment and the consciousness, the person abducted would feel the same sensations as if in the physical body. Many of the abductees report being pulled through solid walls, glass windows and the tops of cars.

Has anyone had the opportunity to check where the physical body is at the time of abduction? Usually those who were with the one taken report having been put into a deep sleep or trancelike state. What do you think?

Astral projection is a useful technique to learn because it can enable you to live life more fully and effectively by gaining a greater awareness from your astral travels. You may need to repeat this procedure several times before you accomplish it. Some people can achieve it on the first try. As with all other metaphysical techniques, positive psychological expectation is a key factor in producing good results. The following technique will focus your attention, ingrain in the subconscious the desire to astrally project, and serve as a dynamic form of autosuggestion.

Technique For Astral Projection:

1. Sit or lie in a comfortable position.

2. Take a few deep breaths, relaxing more and more with each breath.

3. Visualize a candle flame.

4. Keep staring at the flame.

5. Become one with the flame.

6. Feel very sleepy ... feel a deep heaviness all over.

7. Don't go to sleep, just let your breathing become deeper.

8. Block everything from your mind except astral travel.

9. Say these words three times: "I am traveling in the astral but I am aware of all that I see and do. I will recall everything when I am back in my physical body.

10. Will your astral body to leave its physical counterpart.

11. Feel the astral body withdrawing, like a cork rising out of water.

12. Feel a tingling sensation.

13. The tingling ceases and a coolness comes over you.

14. Now you feel an electrical shock as your astral body lifts from your physical body.

15. Keep your eyes closed, even though you can see your physical body where you left it.

16. Keep your thoughts within the room for the first few flights.

17. Take one last look at your body. Look around the room and then return to your physical body.

CHAPTER FIVE

Ultimate Power-Pak

Have you ever wished you had a power source you could call upon when you needed more energy than you could muster? You have such a supply at your command. One overworked writer/publisher followed these instructions and was astounded at such energy! He termed it "miraculous."

Please, do not waste this store of energy by using alcohol, tobacco, heavy foods and negative thinking. This resource is too precious to squander. Guard your thoughts. Build positive, productive ideas; ways to enrich the lives of those you love. You deserve to be rich, happy and successful.

This power-pak will aid you in attaining whatever you desire. But power is power-*ful* and as you indulge in metaphysical principles, you must realize that this practice carries with it a responsibility. Be wise and frugal where this power is concerned. It is an impersonal force; it does not care whether you use it for good or evil. The responsibility is yours.

A metaphysical path must be traveled with caution. The same power that will bring you your heart's desire will also drive you down if misused. Energy misdirected is still energy.

If you focus your energy into negative thoughts it could be catastrophic! Your temper, if unbridled, will be more savage. Negative thoughts and words drain you and they have a way of materializing.

What we refer to as miracles are only metaphysical principles that are carried out in accordance to Universal Laws, using this same power source. These miracles come about as a result of positive energy flow. But it is all the same power. There are many ways to build, store, use and misuse this tremendous power.

In my metaphysics class, I asked my students to think of something they desired, but were unable to achieve. They were instructed to use metaphysical techniques for visualization, meditation and for increasing their energy levels. I told them that they must see the desired objective as though it had already materialized. This must be done twice a day; upon arising and when going to sleep (while one is in the astral state). If a negative thought arose, they were to say with authority, "Cancel."

One student, a nurse by profession, had the wish to rid herself of a very large debt. After following my instructions religiously for two weeks, Jane called me asking, "Would God cheat?"

I assured her that indeed, "He could not!"

Here is her story. Having done her exercises, meditation and visualization for two weeks, she proceeded to a store to make her usual monthly payment. The clerk, to her surprise, assured her that she owed the store nothing.

Upon her insistence, the manager was called. He examined the books and agreed with the clerk that she did not owe this store anything.

She momentarily forgot that this was exactly the outcome she had desired. She was so intrigued by the vanishing debt that she just had to know what happened!

"Bring out the other books," she demanded, "I must know what happened to that awful debt that has kept me strapped for so long!"

"We have no other books, except those in the warehouse," the manager said.

"What do you do with those books?" she asked, bewildered.

"We keep them for seven years according to the tax law and then burn them. But we do not look at them, ever."

Jane insisted, "I must know what happened! The bill I owe this store has been a tremendous burden. How can it just disappear? Can't you see why I must know?"

By this time the manager was perturbed with Jane. "Please, madam. It would cost far too many man-hours to satisfy your curiosity."

She was perplexed. She threatened to write the store owner and tell him that the manager refused to let her pay her bill. He saw he was defeated and finally gave in.

"Madam, I am going to give in to your demands, in spite of my better judgment, even though it will cost this store far more in manpower than the debt you think you owe. We'll have to search the warehouse. What a millstone!"

Several days passed. The manager called. It seems that after searching diligently, they had found, down on the last page of the ledger, almost illegible, the sum she owed the store.

Jane called me. "If, as you say, God cannot cheat, explain to me how this store would not lose because of this error?"

"Jane," I answered, "Do you really believe that a God who can balance this globe so tenuously on its axis, that if it is off a fraction, one way or the other, everything on this planet will either freeze solid or be burned to a crisp by the sun; He cannot account to one store for your bill?"

"Now, I have that horrible debt in front of me again! What happened?" She exclaimed.

"You asked for a miracle. He gave it to you and you threw it back in His face. The wages of sin is death. Oh, not as we think of death but it was the death of your miracle, wasn't it?" I explained.

Now, I will share with you, my readers, my own example of how this metaphysical power can drive you down if you allow negativity to enter your life. I have been teaching metaphysical principles for years; so you know I knew better.

This negative happening kept me in its power for ten long agonizing years.

I kept a ready supply of stored energy at all times. This experience caught me by surprise. I had not considered that someone outside myself could affect my life so forcefully, especially one I loved dearly. This person's action sent me hurling down that negative path so fast and furiously that it took me ten years to gain control. Like attracts like, and I had a rush of negatives that wouldn't stop! The power I had accumulated, drove me down like a pile driver!

I became negative, so I attracted negative people and circumstances. It was like a snow ball rolling downhill, gathering as it went, taking me with it! After losing about $250,000, like Job in the Bible, I realized that, "The thing I most feared had come upon me!"

During my downward plunge, I had gotten into a terrible marriage, which proved costly; financially, physically and emotionally. This, along with bad business ventures and the negative people I had attracted, had to be turned around. How could I attract positive results when I was wallowing in the negativity of fear and remorse?

I knew that to turn the tide, all I had to do was to have one thing turn around and all else would follow. Taking full responsibility for my plight, I began my long road home. Thank God, I knew the way! I thought, "How can one, who knows the law, get so buried in the mire of negativity that he is blind to its principles?"

The prodigal son was down to feeding with the swine when he realized his plight was of his own making. He said, "My father is rich! I must arise and go to my father." The father saw him coming, and ran to embrace him! Even though his father had been heartbroken when his son left, notice that the father did not try to keep the son from leaving. This was the son's own free will. He gave him the right to go or stay, to think positively or negatively, to stay in lack or accept prosperity!

God promised Abraham (who represents all of us) that, "Whatever you see, I promise it to you."

What a wonderful promise; anything we see! God did not say it has to be a good thing we see—whatever we see! If we see poverty, it is promised to us. And if we see riches, it is promised to us. We are truly the captain of our own ship!

I was looking at all the terrible things that I was experiencing, forgetting what I had taught to others. I had to change my way of thinking to change my world. I became my own counselee.

I would have to change the picture in my mind and begin to see the desired results instead of what was happening around me. I had to see the completed picture of what I wanted my life to be like; to see and act as though it had already materialized, just as I had taught. I thought, "Physician, heal thyself!"

The path was not an easy one; far from it. I began to

remember how it was when I was teaching and living metaphysical principles; the miracles and outworking of Universal Law.

I knew that ignorance of the law, or forgetting it for a time does not exempt one from its recompense. I had been reaping exactly what I was sowing—negativism! I needed to see that, and do some constructive, positive visualization to set those metaphysical principles in motion.

I began, one at a time, to forgive those who had wronged me, and to forgive myself for allowing the hurt. Then I determined that the grief I had suffered had to account for something. I realized it was a life lesson; a learning experience. I began serious meditation, prayer and practice of metaphysical ethics.

We must guard our thoughts. We must see only what we want, instead of looking at what we don't have. Don't ever state an affirmation or visualize a beautiful thing and then let in a negative thought. That is like writing something and immediately erasing it. You might as well not write it.

Make your thoughts something you would like to materialize in your life. Be on guard that someone or something, like in my experience, does not set you hurling down that negative path. It could take you years to set things right again.

Depression, anger, jealousy, fear and worry can rob you of the success you could have had. If someone is trying to get you on a downward path through anger or wrongdoing, stop and say to yourself, "I behold the God in you." Or use any words you like, The Divine Power, Universal Intelligence; whatever works for you.

I remember a story of a man being held at gun point in a dark alley. As the thief demanded his money, the man said, "I behold the God in you."

After several attempts to rob him and the man reiterating "I behold the God in you," the culprit ran down the alley shouting over his shoulder, "You're crazy!" The Divine works in mysterious ways.

If you are in need of money, bless your wallet, your bank book and your monthly bills. Hold them in your hand and state this affirmation, "I bless these bills and the service they provide. I send them forth with joy and my good returns to me magnified." Bless your money and checkbook the same way.

A young salesman was telling me that he needed more money. I had him do the aforementioned exercise. Then I blessed his business card and asked him to keep it near him as a reminder of the good coming to him; to look at the card often and repeat the affirmation.

Within a month, he called to tell me that he was top salesman for the month. Three months later, he had bought a new car. The next call revealed that he had earned the position of manager. Finally, he called to tell me that he had moved into a new house and was leaving on a luxurious vacation.

A year passed. He called to ask if he could come by and have me bless his business card for another year. He exclaimed, "I have had so many blessings. I want to continue this practice for the rest of my life."

"Why don't you bless the card yourself, the same way you bless your wallet and bank book?" I asked.

"Are you telling me it will work if I do the blessing? I thought it worked so well because you blessed my business card."

I answered, "Jim, the same Universal Intelligence that resides in me lives in you. It was not I, but your faith in your good that brought about all these miracles."

I didn't hear from Jim for a while. Then he called to ask if it would be alright to share this secret with his friend who was down on his luck. I assured him that he should share it with him and any others who might need it.

If one has enough faith to believe in the outcome without a symbol such as a blessed card, a rabbit's foot, or an amulet, fine. But if you need a token, so be it!

If you are a student of metaphysics, you might use your "Ultimate Power-Pak!"

Technique for the Ultimate Power-Pak

1. Sit erect, not tense.

2. Take a deep breath as you silently count to five.

3. As you breathe in, close your jaws and clench your fists; visualize the breath bringing to you, surges of energy which you are storing within yourself.

4. Relax as you exhale to the count of ten.

5. Repeat this procedure rhythmically, ten times.

Within 20 minutes you will feel great! For even more effect you may add the following: **"Child of the Sun"** technique.

1. Sit erect but relaxed, feet touching, hands clasped.

2. Visualize the sun, a flaming orb of energy!

3. Focus your mind on your head. Visualize a line leading to the sun.

4. Mentally lift your consciousness from the body

and follow this line in spirit that leads to the ball of fire. Proceed to the sun. Let the energy of the sun flow through you. Feel like Peter Pan, flitting around in this prodigious orb of energy. You are a child of the sun; there is nothing to fear. Let this invigorating, strengthening power engulf your entire spirit. After one minute you must return to your body.

You will be reluctant to leave but you must. More than one minute would afford you so much energy, you would not be able to sleep. Do this only during early morning hours. This burst of energy will last for hours.

AUDREY CRAFT DAVIS

CHAPTER SIX

. . . .

I've Got
Your Number

Numerology is the science of numbers. It is an easy and fun way to explore the mysteries of the human psyche. Numbers are everywhere. Birth dates, credit cards, your social security number; they form a language all their own. Learn to decode this language and all kinds of new information about your career, love life, family and friends, becomes available to you.

Numerology was invented by the ancient Babylonians. The Greeks and Persians improved on their theories, and the Romans advanced the science even further. Today, numerologists use the simplified, alphabetical code. It is based on the theories of Pythagoras, a Greek Mystic and Mathematician born about 550 BC. He believed the world was built on the power of numbers.

Numerology is one of the oldest psychic sciences. It is said that numbers were here before letters. Even before we had language, we could count. We were able to distinguish between one stick or two. We could count on our fingers. We were able to determine the number of days until the next full moon.

In a way, numbers found us. They have always existed. Numbers exist outside the specific influences of climate, location and history. In other words, unlike language, numbers cannot be influenced by culture. The idea of *five* is the same to all of us, no matter where we are, or what language we speak. The same cannot be said for the idea of *house*. A person living in the Steppes, in Eurasia, two hundred years ago, has a very different understanding of the concept of *house* than say, someone living in New York City today. Numbers have a universal history. They are part of the Divine laws that govern everything.

You are a series of numbers. Such as: your birth date, name, social security, licenses, passports, credit cards, phone, residence, and dates you travel. You can learn much about yourself, your family, and friends by knowing how to find the numerical value of these numbers and what they say about a particular area of your life.

I was doing a numerology report for a gentleman when I noticed that every number that had anything to do with his car, such as his driver's license, his license tag, inspection sticker, and registration, was a five.

I said to him, "You really love to drive, don't you?"

He was astounded that I could know so much about him by using numbers. Then I explained that the number 5 represents excitement and travel.

My husband and I do a lot of traveling. We check our numbers concerning the day we begin and end any trip or cruise. We also check the cabin or room number, our table reservation, any numbers associated with the trip. If a number five shows up for our table, we know our dinner companions will be exciting people to be with. If we come up with a lot of sevens, we will expect something mysterious or mystical.

A comprehensive understanding of numerology requires time and research. There are whole volumes dedicated to the specifics of numerology and can be found in any local library. These books devote entire chapters to just one number. You'll find in-depth analysis in these books and various techniques for finding answers to a great many questions. Here are a few techniques to get you started.

Numerology Technique For Finding Your Birth Number

The following method will teach you how to read your birth numbers: First, take a sheet of paper and write the day, month and year of your birth. Next, translate each into a number using this table:

January = 1	February = 2	March = 3
April = 4	May = 5	June = 6
July = 7	August = 8	September = 9
October = 10	November = 11	December = 12

Add the numerical value of the day, month and year of your birth number. Always reduce the number to a single digit. If the number you end up with is 18, then add the 1 and the 8 together. $1 + 8 = 9$. Example: June 7, 1920 equals the numerical value of June (which is 6) plus the value of the day (7) plus the 4 digits of the year. Reduce to the common denominator; a single digit number: $(1 + 9 + 2 + 0)$ $=12$. $1 + 2 = 3$. Now total the three numbers: $6 + 7 + 3 = 16$.

$1 + 6 = 7$. Seven is the birth number, which never changes. Your lucky day is the same as your birth number.

Technique For Finding Your Name Number

The following table will tell you the numerical value of each letter. Use this table to find your name number. Note the value of each letter as follows:

A	B	C	D	E	F	G	H	I
J	K	L	M	N	O	P	Q	R
S	T	U	V	W	X	Y	Z	
1	2	3	4	5	6	7	8	9

Or you may find this chart easier to use:

A J S = 1	B K T = 2	C L U = 3
D M V = 4	E N W = 5	F O X = 6
G P Y = 7	H Q Z = 8	I R = 9

Example: Andrew Smith:

Andrew equals $1 + 5 + 4 + 9 + 5 + 5 = 29$.

Smith equals $1 + 4 + 9 + 2 + 8 = 24$.

Now for a single digit on each name:

Andrew equals 29, then $2 + 9 = 11$ or $1 + 1 = 2$.

Smith equals 24, then $2 + 4 = 6$.

Now add the two digits 2 plus 6 equals 8.

Andrew Smith's name number is 8.

By using these charts you can find the value of any number or word. The number must always be brought to its common denominator of one digit.

Colors also have numerical values as follows:

Black = 1	Yellow = 2	Purple = 3	Orange = 4
Blue = 5	Green = 6	Grey = 7	Red = 8

Gold is a mixture of orange and grey (4 + 7 = 11). Bring to single digit 1 + 1 = 2. So Gold is a 2.

Here is an example of what you might learn about your friend by knowing her favorite color. Let's say her favorite color is blue. Now look at your numerical value of blue on the chart. It is 5. This number 5 tells us that your friend likes excitement and travel. She would be fun to be with.

Some numbers remain constant while others might change during your lifetime. Your birth date can't change so it remains constant. If you marry or add or delete a middle initial, it would change your name number. Your residence and phone number would change if you move. Most numerologists prefer that the name number should be the way you would sign an important paper, such as a check. Many actors change their name in order to have a more favorable number.

Technique For Finding Your Present Year Number

Your birth number indicates your personality type and is unchangeable. Your name number represents ambition and achievement, but it can change.

Each year the numerical vibrations change. This means that when you compute your year number, you use the current year and your birth date. Each year you have a new number and new vibration.

Add the numerical value of your birth date, and the present date.

1995 equals 1 + 9 + 9 + 5 which equals 24, or 2 + 4 equals 6. 1995 is a 6 year.

Add your birth and name number to the present year

(1995). If your birth number is 5 and your name number is 6, add 5 + 6 + 6 =17 or 1 + 7= 8. Your personal year is 8. Use the description section to locate your present year number and see what's in store.

Have you ever wanted to know how others see you? To find out, add all the consonants in your name, reduce that number to a single digit and look up the meaning on the chart. To find a suitable mate, do the numerology as you did for yourself. Always remember to reduce each number to one digit and then look up the meaning of that number. Another helpful technique for finding a loving partner is to compute your vibration number by adding all the vowels in your name and reducing them down to a single digit number. Then compare it to your partner's number. You can find out about a person's innermost desire using the same technique. Add all the vowels in their name and then reduce it down to a single digit.

What type of day will you have? Take the date you have in mind. For example, June 9, 1991 = (1 + 9 + 9 + 1 = 20, 2 + 0 = 2). 6 + 9 + 2 =17. Reduce to single digit 1 + 7 = 8. Look up the meaning of 8. For your personal day, add your birth number, name number, and the number of the present day. Reduce it to a single digit. Look for the meaning of the number. Use the following chart to find the meaning of each number.

1 Through 9: What Do They Mean?

Number 1 represents a pioneering spirit. A person who is a one is a loner, a leader, and independent. The number one came first, it stands alone. Often a one can be controlling. They want things done their way. Fortunately, their way is usually the best way. A person whose number is one could give good counsel in helping others help themselves. If your personal day is a one, take advantage of things that fall on a one day. One is good for new beginnings and challenges. Ones are very generous when it comes to love. They tend to focus a lot of attention on their partner. Once a one makes up their mind there are no other choices. October and November are the best months for a one.

Number 2 stands for balance, as well as contrast. Two signifies day and night, negative and positive, seeing both sides of a question. Twos are very loyal. They're empathic and this can lead them to lose sight of their own needs. If you are a two, try to give as much attention to yourself as you do to others. Two signifies good organizational skills. Twos can look at a situation and see what needs to be done. A two day is good for making decisions, weighing problems, and planning. A two may tend to be a little needy in love. The contrasting forces working within them create a balance, a stillness. They look to others to move them along. August is the best time of year.

Number 3 symbolizes intellect. Three is a person who, unlike a two, has a constant drive toward motion. Three represents the triangle, which symbolizes past, present, and future, a beginning, middle and end. It also represents height, depth and breadth; dimension— without which no material thing can exist. Threes are very lucky people. They are full of life. Threes can be excellent leaders. A three lover is very flirtatious and they enjoy adventure in romance. A three day is good for selling, showing off; self-expression, but be careful when signing your name to anything on this day. High summer is your best time of year.

Number 4 represents dependability, endurance, and solidity, as shown by the square. Fours are very pragmatic. They need order. They are not inspired by flights of fancy. The tried and true method works best for any one with this number. Four is the most primitive of all numbers, representing the seasons and the elements: fire, air, earth and water. Four represents the physical realm. Fours love physical affection. A four day is good for routine matters and finishing small jobs. It is not a good day for speculating. Don't do any wagering on a four day. Spring is a great time of year for any four.

Number 5 loves change, excitement, travel, and the abundant life. Fives are enthusiastic and will try anything once. They seek out the new, then move on. They can talk about anything, they love music; they're the perfect date. But long term romance may not be best for a five. A five day is teemed with excitement and vigor; a day for taking chances, if the goal is worth the risk. April and May are good months if this is your number.

Number 6 is honest and reliable. A six is a very steady person. They're sincere, cheerful, and optimistic. They are very capable employees. Sixes are very family oriented. The home and hearth are their favorite places to be. They seek out stable long-term relationships. A six day is a time for goodwill and understanding. It's a good day for a new enterprise. Six represents the six colors of the rainbow. Six is divisible by even or uneven numbers, which makes it a day that depends on you for the outcome. Winter is the best time.

Number 7 stands for healing and helping others. This is

a spiritual number and has religious value. Persons of this number love meditation, study, and research on the higher plane. A seven can tap into the universe and the strange world beyond the mortal veil. A person assigned this number feels that the only sin is cruelty, and the main virtue, kindness. Number seven symbolizes the seven days of the week, seven governing planets, and the seven notes of a musical scale. Seven combines the unity of one with the perfection of six to form its symmetry. Sevens are very sensual beings. Strange things happen on a seven day; things of a mysterious and mystical nature. Early spring is your best time.

Number 8 stands for success and reaping the harvest you have sown. Eight is a number of solidity, as shown by the double square. An eight person has a way of getting the best out of others, but has a tendency to judge others by their wealth and success. Eights have strong psychic abilities. They are often very attractive and get a lot of attention from the opposite sex. An eight day is suited for solid investments and decisions associated with finance. The middle of the year is a very good time for you.

Number 9 is the greatest of all numbers, representing consciousness, unity, and grand achievement. A nine person can excel in music, art, and invention. Nines are visionaries. They see beyond the present moment and accomplish great things in the long term. Their vision leads them into dark places sometimes, and they tend to question the nature of those around them, especially their lovers. A nine day is good for presenting proposals. It's a day for personal triumphs, and artistic and competitive projects. On a nine day, aim for higher things. Use your higher mind to guide all your decisions. If you are fair and good natured, great things can happen. The months of July and August are great if you're a nine.

My husband and I have been convinced of the power of numbers by studying this fascinating science. Many great teachers and leaders, past and present are equally confident of the power in numbers. Numerology gives us the tools to explore our deepest personal desires, dreams, and challenges. Life should be a continual awareness, alive with self-expression and freedom. Numerology is an easy method you can use to answer important questions and change your life. Try it and see if numerology might add an exciting dimension to your life.

CHAPTER SEVEN

Is It My Right To Prosper?

We live in a universe overflowing with abundance, yet so many people seem to experience lives filled with lack and limitation. Can it be that only a fortunate few are destined for prosperity?

The answer to that question is "No." Abundance and prosperity is your birthright. You are a part of the Divine; as such, you have all the powers, qualities and attributes of the Divine essence within you. You are one with the Creative Power of the Universe, which lacks nothing. All the wealth of the universe is within you. It is only fear that says there is not enough to go around, so *someone* has to suffer. Such an attitude divides people, promoting competition and negativity.

The ultimate goal is spiritual well-being; what is experienced on the spiritual level is reflected in the material level. There is no virtue in poverty. Nowhere do the Masters teach that it is a vice to be rich and a virtue to be poor. In the ancient teachings, if someone was in lack, the question was "where have you sinned?" None of the great Masters believed that poverty or ill health was a blessing to anyone, or that it served any good purpose.

No one needs to be poor. Poverty has no power to help anyone. Jesus was not poor. He was clad in a fine seamless garment. It was so valuable that the Roman soldiers cast lots for it. A seamless garment was worn by only the well-to-do. Modern scholars agree that Jesus was honored and sustained far better than most Rabbis of that age. He was well clothed, housed, and fed. He knew the secret of supply, and he placed the Divine source first as his ultimate and inexhaustible resource.

Poverty can be defined as a state of lack, destitution, or deficiency. None of the great Masters advocated poverty. Study the teachings of Buddha, Jesus, Mohammed or Krishna. Their teachings stress the need to resign from worldly sensations. The key though is to resign from the "love of" such sensations. Such "love" diminishes you because you are more focused upon the "love object"—in this case money and riches—rather than the role it should play in your life.

Prosperity is the state of being successful, acquired through a combination of diligence, faith and attitude. Who makes the decision as to which one will be rich and which one will be poor? As agents of free will, we make the choice.

Words and thoughts are things. They materialize! We begin with pictures in our mind, which are transformed into actions. If you see poverty, you become it. If you see riches, they will indeed come to you. We are all endowed with free will—we may choose what is in our world. What you cannot envision cannot be yours. The riches of your mind know no limitations but those which you impose on yourself.

Emmet Fox says it this way. "Every time we use or imply the word, 'I' or 'I am,' we are drawing a check on the universe. The check will be cashed and the proceeds will come to us." If we say, "I am a failure or I am poor, I am ill," the check will be cashed and the proceeds of failure, poverty or ill health will be paid to us. But if our words are, "I am rich, healthy and a success," our dividends will be success, good health and prosperity. Ignorance of the law does not negate its recompense.

If there is a lack of prosperity in your life, perhaps you should consider what kind of seed you are sowing, what thoughts are dominating your life. Recognize your own responsibility for your life's experiences and set a new course in motion.

We are constantly decreeing something to the universe, either consciously or unconsciously. With every thought, we are either increasing or diminishing the good in our lives. We live in a universe of inexhaustible substance, which is ready to manifest itself according to our thoughts.

Substance comes into expression through the mind of man. Every man who has ever prospered has done so by the precepts of Universal Law, for that is the only way. Many have not even known that they were using universal principles, yet once the law was set into motion, they reaped the benefit of its unfailing action. Supply comes to us in accordance with our ability and desire to use it.

Another secret of living a joyously abundant life is to want success and riches for others as much as you want them for yourself. Instead of praying for money, you might ask for rich ideas that might help others or enrich our planet.

Tithing is one of the best means to increase your substance. Tithe comes from an Old English word meaning "one-tenth."

It is one of the fundamental laws of life; after the harvest, the farmer's tithe is one-tenth of his crop, which he gives back to the soil. Without such a tithe, there would be no crop and no harvest. Tithing sets the law of gratitude in motion. Gratitude keeps you attuned to the infinite, connected with the creative forces of the universe.

As your wealth expands, so does your tithe. It does not have to necessarily be one-tenth; it should be what you can give cheerfully, freely, and with a sense of abandonment, knowing that the Universal Intelligence is your source of supply, thereby assuring that your needs are met at all times.

When you give freely and joyously the soul gains strength and confidence. Do not begrudge your tithes; fear of shortage negates the purpose of tithing and such an attitude will attract lack to you and prevent the blessings of abundance from flowing to you. It is better to give nothing than to give grudgingly. Instead, bless your tithe and release it, and it will return to you a thousandfold. You will become a magnet, attracting prosperity and abundance into your life.

Tithing does not have to be only money; you may also tithe your time, talent and thoughts. Giving and receiving, whether of tangibles or intangibles, is like a river. As long as there is an inlet as well as an outlet, the water flows pure, but if the river gets damned up from lack of circulation, the water stagnates. We receive to give and we give to receive.

Sow seeds of plenty in your life and keep the atmosphere charged with joy and thanksgiving. Use the law of gratitude to increase your prosperity. As I stated in chapter five, when you receive a bill, bless the goods or service it represents. Bless your cash, your bank account and your wallet. Use the following affirmation:

"I bless this money and these bills which represent my

comfort. I send this money forth with joy and it returns to me multiplied. I am grateful for the ever-increasing flow of abundance in my life." The best time to do this is at bed time and upon awakening.

Concentrate on all the good you have done—the times you gave when you really couldn't afford to give; when you helped a stranger with no thought of reward; when you were especially understanding to your children and family—and realize that you must receive in accordance to the universal law of attraction.

If you concentrate upon lack, that is what you will attract; thinking and feeling abundant will bring more abundance into your life. Know that the infinite wealth of the universe will flow unstintingly to you. Develop the consciousness of abundant living and you have to receive. It is the way of Divine Mind. It is your right to prosper!

Technique To Reap Prosperity

1. Do this upon awakening and just before sleeping. Get into a comfortable position.

2. Breathe deeply and rhythmically. Relax as you focus on your breathing.

3. Release all feelings of remorse, thoughts of being cheated, of being unappreciated, of using poor judgment or of wondering how to get even. Release all these thoughts to the Divine. As they try to invade your consciousness say affirmatively, "Cancel."

4. Think of all the good you have done, the blessings you have brought into the lives of others.

5. With a deep realization of the Universal Law

at work in your life, realize that you have a tremendous harvest, just waiting for you to reap it.

6. Feel the richness of the harvest; ripe and ready for your harvesting.

7. Plan what you will do with the bountiful reward. Who will you want to share it with?

8. State, "I claim my good of past and present. I accept my blessings. I welcome them. My good is at hand and I experience it, now!"

9. End with seeing a rich harvest. See it NOW!

10. Do this morning and night. Then let it go until next time.

CHAPTER EIGHT

Mastery of Psychic or Soul Energy

We live in a sea of absolute energy, a life energy or force that is found in all things. We are surrounded by it in the same way a fish is surrounded by water. It is part of everything that exists: earth, air, water, fire, the planets and constellations, even our own consciousness. This energy can also be called *psychic* or *soul* energy.

Psychic energy functions at an extremely high vibrational rate. We can detect this Universal life force as it emanates from all things; even inanimate objects. It is *the* primordial life force and through it, we become connected to the rest of the universe.

Think of your soul as a tiny electromagnetic transmitter. Every thought you think, every action and reaction, is broadcast out among the cosmic airwaves. Once there, it has access to everything in the universe.

Because everything in the universe has a life field, all the fields affect and are affected by all other life fields. There is a constant interchange of energy going on all the time. All experience involves this exchange of energy. So you can see how important it is to make a positive contribution to this shared psychic energy field.

We need to learn to use this psychic energy correctly in order to better our world. As we become more attuned to the psychic energy of the planet, we will enter into a spirit of loving cooperation with the natural world, functioning as equals and co-creators rather than subjugators and exploiters. We need to overcome the idea of "dominion" over the planet and learn to cooperate with nature. Our selfishness has lead to the exploitation of the environment by science and technology and thus contributed to air and water pollution, overpopulation and other ecological threats.

Improper use of psychic or soul energy can have disastrous consequences. The history of war is the history of misused soul energy. Wars cannot be fought without a great many people focusing on the destruction of battle. What a waste of our priceless psychic energy. These expenditures of misdirected soul energy have had devastating effects on the life of our planet and the future of humanity. There are many ways to waste and misuse this valuable energy, among them jealousy, greed, selfishness and all the other fear-based emotions.

The important thing is to recognize that this energy connects everything together. We are all One. We can use our psychic energy to affect positive change and bring peace and harmony to our planet.

One way to accumulate psychic power is by communing with nature. Touch the tip of your fingers and thumb to the points of pine needles on a fir tree. Hold them there about two minutes. Do this several times a day and you will definitely see an increase in your feeling of well-being. You may also recharge your batteries in one 20 minute session, or longer if you so desire. Taking a nap beneath a pine tree, and leaning against its trunk will enable you to tap into the tree's life force. This is very beneficial because pine trees contain much of this psychic life force. Other trees that are good for this purpose are oak, beech and apple trees.

I knew of a terminally ill man whose doctors had done all they could for him, and gave him only a short time to live. The man went to a national park where there was a dense pine forest. Going to the very center of the forest, he pitched his tent and camped there for six months. During that time, he asked the trees to share their energy with him, and he worked hard to rid himself of any negative soul energy. When he returned, his doctors were astounded— there was no trace of his illness. It was completely gone.

The Aura

The aura is the electromagnetic energy field that surrounds all living things and inanimate objects. The source of this energy field is psychic or soul energy. The human aura is three dimensional as it surrounds the body and is composed of different layers of energy. Each layer has it's own vibrational rate. The finer and more subtle the vibration, the larger the layer and the more space it occupies.

The first layer of the human aura surrounds and supports the physical body; it is called the astral or etheric body. The next field is affected and changed by what we feel and is appropriately called the emotional field. The third, the mental field, is controlled by our thoughts, attitudes and viewpoints. There is a fourth field, the spiritual aura, which can extend to great distances from the physical body, depending on the awareness of the individual. It has been said that Buddha's spiritual aura extended over 200 miles.

Technique For Reading The Aura

To read the aura, you must unfocus your eyes slightly, as though staring but not looking at the person. Actually, this is best accomplished by focusing your eyes about six to nine inches beyond the subject. As the eyes begin to tire, the focus changes to an almost unseeing gaze. Then the aura becomes visible. One might practice on oneself by using a mirror and diffusing the light. Allow some time for this ability to develop, don't force it. Do not strain to see the aura. If you don't succeed right away, keep trying calmly and patiently.

Peracelsus, a Swiss-born alchemist and physician, believed that all illness was a result of a break or a weakness in the aura. By restoring the aura, one's health is returned to normal. Many people still believe this is true, and today, doctors all over the world heal the life force that sustains the physical body rather then the body itself.

The healer examines the aura for any discoloration, or breaks. These may determine what is causing the illness. Then the healer visualizes different colors, depending on the specific illness, and infuses them into the aura of the patient. Violet for soothing, bright green for vigor, orange for a mood elevator, golden-yellow to stabilize and balance agitated nerves, red for stimulation, and clear blue for the blood and organs.

These healers find that rehabilitating another person's energy, by way of their own energy, is just as effective as medicating a physical illness. The healer may use "laying on of the hands" to project his psychic energy into the patient. Or they simply alter their own state of consciousness and focus their subconscious mind on the psychic or soul energy of the patient.

All the functions of the body—physical, metabolic, emotional, mental and spiritual, are affected by the energies we exchange with one another. Have you ever heard of a psychic vampire? A psychic vampire is someone who drains other people's life energy through their auras. Many times, these individuals are unaware that their pessimistic, negative atmosphere is depleting those around them. The rest of us can feel it immediately but we're unable to identify the source. The following is an encounter with a psychic vampire.

I stopped by my friend Geraldine's office to take her to lunch. I noticed that she seemed rather pale and listless. At first I thought about rescheduling our lunch, I thought she might be too tired, but she insisted that all she really needed was some fresh air.

The walk to the cafe was refreshing and as we seated ourselves in the restaurant, her color began to come back and she was her old self again.

When we returned to the office, I ran into Bill, an old friend and chatted in the hall for a few minutes while Geraldine called her secretary Nancy into her office.

Afterwards, I went into Geraldine's office and once again, I noticed that Geraldine was pale and listless. Bill, also seemed tired and drained after talking to the secretary for several minutes. I was positive that the girl was a psychic vampire.

Walking into Geraldine's office, I asked, "How long has Nancy been with you?"

"About six months, I guess. Why do you ask?" She answered.

"I must tell you that you have a psychic vampire in your

midst! I noticed that both you and Bill are depleted after any encounter with her."

"What on earth is a psychic vampire?" Geraldine inquired.

"A psychic vampire is one who saps your psychic energy by draining your aura. Oh, I don't think Nancy realizes it, but she is definitely the reason you and Bill had severe drops in your energy levels. Your physical and mental health is at risk with her around."

I taught Geraldine and Bill to keep a protective white light around themselves at all times when Nancy was nearby. Luckily, Nancy left the company shortly after my visit, and Geraldine is once more her old vibrant self.

So, you can see that it is important to keep your aura strong and healthy. A vibrant aura is a means of protection against the negative thoughts and actions of the people around you. A strong aura will help you feel serene and enable you to focus on the positive. To maintain a strong aura, we need to eat sensibly and get proper rest. A positive mental attitude is essential.

I have been told repeatedly by several psychics that I have a very strong aura. Once, I was waiting for a friend in the lobby of a hotel when I felt someone staring at me— intently. I turned around to see where the strong impression was coming from.

A tall man walked over to me and said, "You must forgive me. I know you sensed me looking at your aura. There are very few truly beautiful auras and yours is so lovely, I just couldn't help myself."

He explained that some auras reflect dark, dingy or ugly colors. This can be due to ill health or a mean or negative temperament.

He went on to explain that his ability to read auras was

the result of a bad fall from a ladder, which had broken his skull. The severe fracture had opened his third eye which resulted in his ability to read auras. After his recovery, his psychic abilities had become quite strong.

We chatted for a few more minutes, then he took his leave of me. After he left, I realized we hadn't exchanged names; yet it had been one of those very comfortable conversations such as occur between two old friends. It wasn't until I read about him later in a magazine that I realized I had been talking with the famous psychic Peter Hurkos.

Technique For Strengthening Your Aura

Here is a simple technique to strengthen your aura. First, picture a cylinder of light about nine feet high and five feet in diameter. Then, visualize yourself suspended in the center. See the light as clear white, with rays of pastels playing through it. Draw into the cylinder spiritual protection by thinking of the Divine consciousness. Use this armor to protect yourself and your loved ones by mentally placing this cylinder of light around them and yourself. Music is a good vibration-builder. I suggest you fill the cylinder with your favorite music either by actually playing it on the stereo, or just imagine the notes in your mind.

Psychic or soul energy can have many uses. The dowser uses this psychic energy to find water, oil, tunnels and ore. The primitive hazel twig has given way to metal or plastic, collapsible Y-shaped devices. Some dowsers use a pendulum and a map.

Physical objects, such as clothing and jewelry, retain the energy vibrations of those who have worn them. People's homes also may retain these vibrations. A psychometrist, by holding an object in their hand or entering a house, can tune into the energy vibrations and read the personality or history of a particular individual.

Other avenues for using this type of power are: telepathy; reading another's mind, teleportation; the ability to move objects without touching them, precognition; seeing or being aware of events before they happen and many other psychic abilities. Or astral projection, which has already been covered in chapter four. Levitation is another psychic feat; defying gravity by lifting oneself or another person into the air by mind power. All of these powerful abilities are accomplished through the use of psychic energy.

If you want to strengthen your psychic or soul energy, keep your brain stimulated by positive mind action. Laziness, whether physical or mental, dissipates this precious life force. Thoughts are power. Don't let your thoughts wander. Gather them to you and control them; remember that where your attention goes, your energy flows.

You can lose much of your energy by focusing on people with a lower vibrational frequency than your own. Instead, learn to focus your thoughts on the great teachers, writers, musicians and spiritual beings. They will inspire you mentally and spiritually. By using the law that says, "Energy follows thought" we can strengthen, heal, and stimulate any part of our bodies.

Color and sound play an important role in our lives and can be used to great advantage. Chants and mantras have been used to increase psychic power for centuries in many countries like China, India and Tibet. The Om sound is considered the highest spiritual vibration and is a powerful mantra, when sounded in D above middle C. When done in groups, the sound produces collective psychic power.

Technique For Increasing Your Psychic Power

Stand in front of an open window and stretch your arms out horizontally. Breathe in to the count of five. Breathe out to the count of ten. Repeat ten times.

This exercise can be done while seated or while walking. Do the counting until you can breathe rhythmically without it. Once a day is good, but two or three is better. After a month you may add the following technique: Sit straight, head erect, feet crossed at ankles, hands clasped, in your lap. Take a deep breath through the nose, counting to eight. Hold the breath in the lungs to the count of twelve. Count ten as you exhale through the nose. Direct the air to the spot where it enters the nasal passage from the throat. Feel vibration at this spot. Repeat five times. Do this exercise three times a day.

After doing these exercises for a few weeks, test your energy: Separate your hands, then bring them close together without touching. Cup the palms and bring each finger close to the corresponding finger on the other hand. Keep them about one half inch apart. Breathe normally. You will feel the energy vibrate at the finger tips. In a dark room you can actually see a bluish haze between your hands—this is your soul energy.

As you master the technique of acquiring, preserving and restoring psychic soul energy, you can begin to focus your mind and direct your thoughts to the higher energy centers or chakras—the heart, head and throat chakras. When these three centers are linked together, they become a triangle of psychic power. The solar plexus center is located between the higher centers and the lower centers. The lower centers are located in the stomach, sex organs and the base of the spine. These already receive too much attention.

You may be so enthusiastic about your success, you may wish to add a mantra, such as the OM. This sound as well as visualizing colors will help stimulate your higher centers.

As you advance to using the following technique, you will begin to change. You will become aware of the thoughts of others. At first, you will think they are your own. You may hear a voice call your name. This means your progress has been observed by higher beings. One of them may become your spiritual teacher or spirit guide.

The following technique incorporates color for effect, to strengthen head, heart and throat chakras:

The Heart: Focus your attention on your heart. See it bathed in a pink cloud. Inhale to the count of seven. Hold the breath to the count of ten as you raise your attention to the head center. See the pink cloud encompass your head as you exhale to the count of seven. Hold the breath out to the count of ten as you visualize the pink cloud enveloping your body.

The Throat: See a blue cloud encircling your throat. Inhale to the count of seven. Raise your attention to the head. See it bathed in a blue cloud as you exhale to the count of ten. Hold the breath out to the count of ten as you visualize your body enveloped in the blue cloud.

The Head: Inhale to the count of seven as you visualize a white cloud embracing the pituitary gland, located between the eyes in the center of the head. Hold the breath to the count of ten as you see the white cloud encircling the pituitary and pineal glands. The pineal is located a little higher in the head than the pituitary, but they are close together. Exhale to the count of seven. See your head encircled in the white cloud. Hold the breath out to the count of ten as you visualize the entire body enveloped in the white cloud. Sound Om three times. Arise and put this all out of your mind.

By using these techniques, you will make real progress in developing your psychic centers. These greatly enhance the speed with which you can gain tremendous amounts of psychic energy.

Choose carefully which of your psychic gifts you wish to work with. You must always center your attention on the good that you can do for the planet and people. Use this power only for good or it can destroy you—it has the ability to drive you down as well as build you up. It is up to you to direct it! Always remember that power is power and brings with it a great responsibility. If you allow yourself to become negative, that negativity will be greatly enhanced.

If you focus on the positive aspects of experience you will find that you have more compassion. You will be able to distinguish the true from the false. Do not be deluded by the passion of the lower centers. Keep your attention on the higher chakras.

Your mind and heart will strive for clearer vision, understanding and humility. You will find yourself developing psychic talents. You will become part of a collective higher consciousness which at this very moment, is working to bring world peace and an end to poverty and suffering.

Technique to Read Auras

1. Seat yourself comfortably and look at the person (or object).

2. Unfocus your eyes slightly, as though staring but not looking at the person. This is best accomplished by focusing your eyes about six to nine inches beyond the subject.

3. As the eyes begin to tire, the focus changes to an

almost unseeing gaze. Then the aura becomes visible.

One might practice on oneself by using a mirror and diffusing the light. Allow the ability to come to you; don't force it. Do not strain to see the aura. If you don't succeed right away, keep trying calmly and patiently.

Technique to Strengthen Your Aura

1. Picture a cylinder of light about nine feet across.

2. Visualize yourself suspended in the center of the cylinder.

3. See the light as luminous white with pastels playing through it.

4. Draw into the cylinder, spiritual protection by thinking of the Universal consciousness.

5. You may play soft music during this exercise. Draw the music into the cylinder.

Technique for Increasing and Preserving Your Psychic Energy

1. Stand before an open window or in the fresh air.

2. Stretch your arms out horizontally.

3. Breathe in to the count of five.

4. Breathe out to the count of ten.

5. Repeat ten times.

After a month of the above exercise, you may add this one:

Alternate Technique

1. Sit straight, head erect, feet crossed at the ankles, hands clasped in your lap.

2. Take a deep breath through the nose, counting to eight.

3. Hold the breath in the lungs to the count of twelve.

4. Count to ten as you exhale through the nose. Direct the breath to the spot where it enters the nasal passage from the throat. Feel the vibrations at this spot.

5. Repeat five times. Do this exercise three times a day.

When you feel you are ready you may add the following chakra exercises.

Heart Chakra

1. Focus your attention on your heart chakra. See it bathed in a pink cloud.

2. Inhale to the count of seven.

3. Hold the breath to the count of ten as you raise your attention to the head center.

4. See the pink cloud encompass your head as you exhale to the count of seven.

5. Hold the breath out to the count of ten as you visualize the pink cloud enveloping your entire body.

Throat Chakra

1. See a blue cloud encircling your throat.

2. Inhale to the count of seven.

3. Raise your attention to the head. See it bathed in a blue cloud as you exhale to the count of ten.

4. Hold the breath out to the count of ten as you visualize your entire body enveloped in a blue cloud.

Crown Chakra

1. Inhale to the count of seven as you visualize a white light encircling the pituitary gland in the center of the head.

2. Hold the breath to the count of ten as you see a white light encircling the pituitary and pineal glands, which are close together.

3. Exhale to the count of seven. See your head encircled in the white light.

4. Hold the breath out to the count of ten as you visualize the entire body enveloped in the white light.

5. Sound Om three times. Arise and put it all out of your mind.

CHAPTER NINE

. . . .

Metaphysical Healing

All healing comes through Divine Energy, Universal Intelligence, God, whatever one chooses to call it. Whether through a surgeon's scalpel, medication, laying on of hands or psychic healing, it is all Divine source. All medicine, whether pharmaceutical or organic, comes from minerals, deposits in the earth, or plant and animal sources. These and even the knowledge of how to properly use them, is from the same Divine Mind.

There are many ways to be healed. Some are not so obvious. Don't be mislead into believing that a healing is some kind of magic trick. It doesn't have to be instantaneous. Many times, a healing is progressive and occurs over a long period of time. Some progressive healings don't even involve doctors or medicine. Many times they involve behavioral changes rather than a specific medical approach. For example, if you start eating different foods, or taking vitamins or getting more exercise, you will feel a pronounced difference in how you feel—body, mind and spirit.

A progressive healing can also start with your individual approach to spirituality. The spiritual approach not only influences the body and mind, it also tends to affect the cosmic forces around you. You may mysteriously start studying positive faith books or begin to listen to subliminal healing tapes. Since your mind is part of Universal Mind, it is no accident that these changes turn you in the right direction.

When you set a goal, whether it be healing or some other endeavor, the Divine part of your mind makes a definite turn towards the accomplishment of that goal. It may be a circuitous route but it will lead directly to the fulfillment of that objective.

Emotion can be a deterrent when it comes to metaphysical healing. It is almost a universal belief that the true measure of our concern for a sick loved one is to cry and show emotion. Metaphysical healing requires us to have a great faith. It is impossible to worry and have faith at the same time. Faith eliminates fear.

The great sages and masters taught that if we have faith, even if that faith is as small as a mustard seed, we could remove mountains; mountains of worry, hate, greed, jealousy and fear. These mountains of fear block the channel to our fulfillment. Negativity must be eradicated.

Never beg the Divine Source for anything. Once a student asked me, "Why is it that I have had no answer to my prayer though I have prayed long and hard for three years."

"You just told me why you haven't had an answer. If you really believed, need you ask more than once? If I offer you something, telling you I wish you to have it, will you reach out and accept it or will you beg me to give it to you?"

Metaphysical healing requires you to believe that the healing you desire has already taken place. This means that you cannot have even the slightest of doubts. Not even a passing worry. Your faith must be so unrelenting and complete that your subconscious cannot accept any other reality. In visualization you are painting a picture of the thing you desire. You must focus your higher mind on this picture and ruminate over all the details. Your picture must be so comprehensive, thorough and complete that your minds eye cannot accept any other reality. Combining visualization and faith is what metaphysical healing is all about.

The technique: First, thank the Divine source for hearing you. Then, ask for the healing. Next, form a picture in your mind of the thing desired. Expect it and feel as though the thing asked for is already yours. Make ready to receive it. You may have to broaden your capacity to receive. You may have to make changes. Be ready if necessary. Finally, all that is left is to accept it and give thanks. I have used this kind of metaphysical prayer many times with great success. The following stories recount how this incredible healing technique has helped me and my family.

The Dream

I was in terribly cold and murky water. It was dark and I could barely see. Suddenly, my two children were there. They were both hurt and I had to keep their heads up above the water to keep them from drowning.

It was hard enough just keeping one of my children afloat. Trying to keep both of them alive was next to impossible. I kept losing them. Physically, I wasn't strong enough. It was clear that the only thing I had to save both my children was the sheer force of my will. Only in truly believing could I accomplish the rescue and succeed.

The next day I had a call. Both of my children, now grown and married, were each in different hospitals. The dream was a foreshadowing. My son had an auto accident and his doctor said there was no hope. My daughter was in a different hospital, for the birth of her son. Both her and the baby's kidneys had failed. Again, there was no hope.

Hard as it was, I knew I dared not go to either hospital. Loving my children as I did, if I saw them in such danger, my fear of losing them could overshadow my praying effectively. Their lives depended on me being able to see the end result I desired; their healing.

I knew that I had to visualize them as The Divine Source's perfect children in spite of what the doctors were saying. I did not dare to falter in my faith for one second. My visualization had to be perfect.

I kept reminding myself that I had to do my part which was to see them as perfect, whole and complete. I thanked the Divine Presence for hearing me. Then I asked for their healing. Next I put a picture in my mind. I visualized my daughter and her husband in the nursery, proudly watching little Josh, as he kicked his legs and threw his arms about. For my son, I visualized him sitting in his living room, telling his wife and children how happy he was to be home with them. My pictures were complete.

I worked at this very hard all day and into the night in order to keep doubt from invading my mind, until I fell into bed exhausted with my pictures clearly ingrained in my consciousness.

I couldn't discuss this tragedy with anyone for they might inject a negative thought into my perfect pictures. I held onto those pictures so close that it took all my strength. It was the hardest thing I had ever done in my life.

During this ordeal, I visited a clairvoyant. I told her nothing.

As I sat down, she exclaimed, "I have never seen such mind control! Hold onto it. You are going to win!"

"Oh, God," I thought, "How I needed that reassurance."

Even though I knew my prayer was being answered, just having one other person know how hard I was working helped.

Though some judged me as being unfeeling, I knew I had done the only thing that would save my loved ones. Of course, my prayer was answered, just as I knew it would be.

Ryan's Eyes

Another example of positive prayer was when my grandson contracted an infection in his eyes. The ophthalmologist looked worried, as he handed my daughter the phone number and address of the best eye specialist in the state.

"I've made arrangements for you to go immediately to his office."

"I don't understand. Why are you sending us to a specialist?"

"I'm afraid your son is losing his eyesight. I want to see if Dr. Lewis will confirm what I have discovered. I hope I'm wrong"

The specialist confirmed it; Ryan was going blind. The disease progressed to where Ryan could barely see at all. He began to study braille. I'll never forget watching Ryan as he was taught to see his mother's face through his fingers so he would remember what she looked like. From the very depths of my soul, I cried out, "No, this cannot be! Ryan's eyes are made of the Divine essence and I know that surely it can heal them.

My family began to visualize Ryan running, riding his

bike, and playing ball, like all the other kids. We continued until his next appointment with his ophthalmologist.

Dr. Lewis was astounded. He could hardly believe his own eyes.

All he could say was, "I don't understand it, Ryan's eyes are perfect. It is a miracle!"

Ryan is now grown and is the proud father of three children and he doesn't even wear glasses.

Jimmy and the X-Rays

My other grandson, Jimmy was hit by a car. His leg was broken, his collar bone was fractured and he suffered a severe skull fracture. The accident had left him deaf and blind. The poor child didn't realize that his parents were right there next to him as he lay in the hospital bed.

He was crying, "I want my mommy and daddy!"

My daughter-in-law was hysterical. I took her aside and told her we must pray for Jimmy's healing; explaining that we must visualize him as healthy.

"How can we do that when he is deaf, blind and has broken bones? He doesn't even know we're here with him."

I explained to her that we must do as we had done for Ryan and see Jimmy as perfect. So, we began to see Jimmy as he was before the accident.

"Remember how Ryan's eyes were healed? We will visualize Jimmy, the same way. Let's see him, his usual boisterous self, when he wakes up in the morning. Let's see Jimmy as the mischievous kid we know him to be. That doctor is going to think he has the wrong X-rays."

This is the most difficult part of any healing. When you see someone you love, in pain or injured, it is close to impossible to look beyond the suffering. It is imperative that we see the solution; not the problem. This takes incredible discipline and faith. Remember, the definition of faith is, "The substance of things hoped for; the evidence of things, not seen."

The next morning, Jimmy woke up the whole ward. He was hungry and he let everybody know it. His hearing was fine. His eyes were healed. The doctor came in to see what all the commotion was about. He rushed out and looked at the original X-rays. Then he made other X-rays.

"How could this be? These can't be the X-rays we made of this child, yesterday...I don't believe it."

The Longest Night

My husband was in the hospital diagnosed with peritonitis. He needed immediate surgery to prevent the poison from spreading. There was only one doctor qualified to do the surgery but he wasn't available until morning and my husband's life hung in the balance.

My daughter had heard the conversation and began to cry, "My daddy is going to die, isn't he?"

When I finally got her quieted, I said, "Honey, the reason the doctor cannot operate tonight, is that the doctor must be at his best, for your father's surgery. Let's see your father as being well, driving his new truck and working in his garden. That's the picture Divine Mind is seeing right now, and all that is asked of us, is that we see it, too. Can you do this for your father?"

She assured me that she could and I sent her home, telling her to go to sleep with this picture in her mind. I kept vigil at my husband's side and visualized that picture all night long.

My husband had the surgery the next day. When the

operation was over the surgeon came out of the O.R. and said, "I never know which is the work of God and which is mine, but we make a great team."

Against all odds, my husband recovered completely.

Distant Healing

In situations where it is impossible to be with the person, distant healing may be the only means. In many cases, it is better that the person does not know you are doing a healing treatment for him or her. If the person is a nonbeliever, that negativity can block the healing.

I had been doing healing treatments for years when I discovered, by accident, about healing the astral or etheric body.

While driving home one night, my husband began to tell me about his son. His son had a very serious condition, it was very painful in his feet, and he suffered all the time. He could not afford to take the time for surgery which would require months in a wheelchair. Listening to my husband speak, a strange feeling came over me. I knew that if I began to do a healing, right there in the car, miles away from my step son, I could heal the boy.

I said, "You know, if I had Charlie's feet in my hands right now, I could heal them," (meaning that Divine Mind, could heal them through me).

Suddenly, I felt as though I actually had Charlie's feet in my hands. My hands began to move over those invisible feet just as I would normally do if he were present. I could feel those awful, thick calluses getting thinner and thinner as I almost mechanically, worked on one foot first, then the other. I continued this treatment until we arrived home. This was a new experience for me. I had never heard of healing the astral (etheric) body.

I said, "Honey, I want you to massage my feet. As I begin to feel the soothing effect of the massage, I want us to transfer the feeling into Charlie's feet." We, together, visualized Charlie relaxing with the massage, and accepting the healing.

The following day, the phone rang. Charlie shouted into the phone, "Dad, you won't believe it. You know how I suffer with my feet constantly...I can't believe this Dad, but I tell you, my feet are well. I haven't done anything for them, it's the darndest thing...how can this be?"

My husband put his hand over the mouthpiece and motioned that he would like to tell his son what had happened, but I whispered a definitive, "No!"

"Why wouldn't you let me tell him?" Louis asked, later.

"How can you be sure Charlie could believe what has happened? His disbelief could reverse his healing. We can't take that chance. Many times the Masters do healings by absentia. I think because they don't want negativity to interfere."

Tiny Prayers

I visited my friend Violet in the hospital and said a prayer for her. The lady in the next bed looked on intently. So I asked a blessing for her, as well. The next day, as I visited, I was not surprised that Violet was better, but I couldn't help noticing a distinct improvement in the lady in the bed next to her. Then I remembered I did say a small prayer for her, too.

Even the tiniest of prayers can be helpful. We can't risk such tiny prayers when attempting a real metaphysical healing. For that, we must be very serious and thorough. Yet, the almost unconscious prayers seem to be very effective. An example of this might be when we hear the shrill of a siren and we murmur a prayer for those in need and for the ones speeding to help.

Recently, while swimming, I overheard a lady say that she was concerned that they would have to pass up Disney World on this vacation because her son was feeling poorly. I thought, "I can help her son feel better."

I said a small prayer. Within five minutes, the child's fever had disappeared and he was having a ball, no sign of illness.

The Cause

Healing can take many forms.

A friend was complaining of arthritis, when I said, "You don't seem the type."

"What do you mean, the type," he inquired.

"Haven't you heard that arthritis can be a resentment disease?" I asked.

"Oh, I don't resent anything," he said thoughtfully as he cupped his chin in his hand, then continued, "Well, maybe I do resent my divorce—it robbed me of my business."

Holding up my finger, I said, "This was caused by resentment of a divorce. I woke up one morning shortly after my divorce with a severe pain in my finger. I was surprised to find the joint all swollen and enlarged."

I went on to tell him how I had resented that my first husband wanted a divorce after pursuing me for a year and a half. I wasn't the one who wanted to get married, and then after I agreed, he decided it wasn't working. I'm not a quitter and I resented that he had made me look like one. I knew that if I didn't get rid of the resentment, all of my fingers would end up this way.

I forgave my husband and then I forgave myself for allowing the resentment. My knotted forefinger (my accusing finger) stands as a reminder to never resent anything.

I remember chatting with a friend whom I had not seen for some time. I was surprised to find that she had developed a severe case of arthritis.

I asked her, "What in the world are you resenting so fiercely?"

She looked rather shocked at my abruptness and started to deny it, but then answered, "I'll tell you. I resent my husband's business, and I resent our long hours. This business is robbing us of the time to be together. We can never go anywhere. Yes, I resent this laundry business," she stated emphatically, as if it were a relief to have finally said it, as she rubbed first one hand and then the other.

"What kind of business would you like to own?" I asked.

She began to describe what it was she really wanted to do; the nursery business. She had studied horticulture and loved flower arranging. It was great to see her face light up as she talked.

"How much pain do you have now?" I asked.

"Well, none. My hands hurt all the time but right now, I have absolutely no pain."

"The pain went along with the need for resentment," I said.

She relayed all that had happened, to her husband. He recognized the need to change their lives and today they own a very successful nursery and my friend is arthritis-free.

I don't say that arthritis is always caused by resentment, but if you should wake up some morning with arthritis-like pains, it might be wise to check it out. Emotional pain can bring on physical pain as well. Finding the emotional connection to that pain may be the first step in healing what ails you.

There is a formula for metaphysical healing: no matter what the cause, the answer is visualization and faith.

Technique For Metaphysical Healing

1. Get very quiet.

2. Relax and focus on your breathing.

3. Relax more and more with each breath.

4. Thank the Divine Source for hearing you.

5. Ask for the healing, forming a complete picture in your mind of the person doing the things he or she would be doing in a healthy condition.

6. Refuse to see the person as incapacitated in any way.

7. Make ready for the healthy person to return home.

8. See a complete picture of the celebration, taking place.

9. Accept it and give thanks.

CHAPTER TEN

Reincarnation: Have We Lived Before?

Have we lived before? Would you like to discover who you were in a past life? Many well-known personalities of all ages, including some of the world's greatest philosophers, writers, musicians, poets, artists, scientists, inventors and statesmen, have believed in reincarnation.

In ancient Greece, there were Pythagoras, Plato and Plotinus. In more recent times, Europeans include Richard Wagner, Gustav Mahler, Paul Gaugin, Wassily Kandinsky, Leonardo da Vinci, Voltaire, James Joyce, Johann Wolfgang von Goethe, Gustave Flaubert, William Butler Yeats, John Milton, William Blake, Percy Bysshe Shelly, Alfred Lord Tennyson, Samuel Taylor Coleridge, George Eliot, George Sand, Albert Schweitzer, Carl Jung, Mohandas Gandhi, and Robert and Elizabeth Barrett Browning. Americans include Benjamin Franklin, Mark Twain, Emily Dickenson, Henry David Thoreau, William James, Ralph Waldo Emerson, Louisa May Alcott, Walt Whitman, Henry Wadsworth

Longfellow, Charles Lindbergh, James Lowell and Henry Ford.

Throughout the history of mankind, in all societies and civilizations, human beings have struggled to find the answers to life's injustice and randomness. The concepts of reincarnation and karma offer an explanation for the seeming inequalities in life. Why is someone born blind? Why is someone born poor, or rich?

Reincarnation is the process by which we return to the earth plane, again and again, in the hopes of advancing to a higher realm of consciousness. To believe in reincarnation is to believe that the soul never dies.

When you die your soul does not die with the physical body. The soul is eternal. It continues living in the etheric or astral world for varying lengths of time, and then chooses to incarnate again on the earth plane.

In these incarnations, the individual soul experiences a variety of different lifetimes, acquires many experiences, and assumes various personalities. Each lifetime affords the soul a variety of lessons. The soul chooses different times, cultures and social backgrounds which enable it to have varied emotional and intellectual experiences. When the lessons are learned and the soul has moved as far as it can, it will graduate to the next level and so on until it leaves the wheel of reincarnation.

Knowing this, would one lie, steal or cheat, just to come back to another life and perhaps pay for, or suffer the same wrong? Our lives are the consequence of our own actions, which arise from our thoughts, speech, and emotions. To believe that we live again gives us a reason in this life for doing our best.

Reincarnation was accepted as a standard belief in all

the ancient civilizations, not only in the Orient but throughout pagan Europe. Various civilizations, such as the Celts,
Hindus, Chinese, Greeks, and Native Americans, all ascribed
to a belief in reincarnation. Belief in the continuity of existence
has been handed down through the myths, legends, sacred
texts, and rituals of many different cultures.

Westerners sometimes find reincarnation hard to accept
because it contradicts many of our Judeo-Christian beliefs.
It was banned by the Christian church, although reincarnation had been a part of early Christian doctrine.

In A.D. 553, the Second Council of Constantinople laid
down the following decree: "Whosoever shall support the
mythical doctrine of the preexistence of the soul and the
consequent wonderful [impossible] opinion of its return,
let him be anathema." Those who had previously been
thought of as saints and founders of Christianity, were de-
clared heretics and officially excommunicated from the
church.

Why did the early Christian church eliminate reincarnation from their religious dogma? Because it took power
from the priests and churches and gave it to the individual,
emphasizing personal responsibility, freedom of choice and
the individual's capacity to create his own destiny. The moral
implications inherent in the law of reincarnation and karma
lead us inescapably to this conclusion: We ourselves are the
only ones responsible for our life situation, whether it be
good or bad.

Have you been somewhere or met someone, knowing
you have never been there nor known that person; yet it all
seemed so familiar? In his book, *Earthly Purpose*, Dick
Sutphen, a well-known past-life regressionist, tells of a civilization at Teotihuacan whose society rivaled the grandeur

of ancient Rome. He speaks of a secret Atlantean Circle and their vows to reincarnate back on earth every 700 years. This civilization lasted for 1000 years.

It is Sutphen's belief that there are 25,000 of this group living on earth at present. After the publication of his book, additional independent discoveries at the Teotihuacan archaeological site provided powerful and accurate support for Dick's report.

Journalist John Walters writes: "Acceptance of the theory of karma and rebirth will settle many problems regarding life which previously seemed insoluble. It brings a reasonable explanation to circumstances and events, to the tragedies and comedies of life that otherwise would make the world seem one vast madhouse or the plaything of a crazed deity."

In a conversation with a friend, composer Gustav Mahler said, "We all return; it is this certainty that gives meaning to life and it does not make the slightest difference whether or not in a later incarnation we remember the former life. What counts is not the individual and his comfort, but the great aspiration to the perfect and the pure which goes on in each incarnation."

Louisa May Alcott, author of *Little Women*, in a letter to a friend wrote, "I think immortality is the passing of a soul through many lives or experiences; and such as are truly lived, used, and learned, help on to the next, each growing richer happier and higher, carrying with it only the real memories of what has gone before."

General George Patton believed that he was a soldier in many other lifetimes. He was a soldier in ancient Troy and a knight in the Crusades; he served with the Stuarts in Scotland, and was Marshal for Napoleon. During his command in

Langres, France, when a soldier volunteered to show him around, he answered that it would not be necessary. He knew it from another lifetime.

Novelist Joan Grant writes,"...seven books of mine have been published as historical novels which to me are biographies of past lives..."

The great German poet and dramatist Johann Wolfgang von Goethe said, "Human genius in a lightning flash of recollection can discover the laws involved in producing the universe, because it was present when those laws were established. I am certain I have been here a thousand times before, and I hope to return a thousand times more."

The renowned composer Richard Wagner, in a letter to a friend, wrote, "In contrast to reincarnation and karma all other views appear petty and narrow. Only the profoundly conceived idea of reincarnation could give me any consolation, since that belief shows how all at last can reach complete redemption."

Each one of these great thinkers believed in reincarnation. The laws of death and rebirth became useful tools in their discoveries about life and love.

Many times seemingly insoluble problems in this life can be traced to patterns set up in past lives. Morris Netherton refers to the *somatic bridge*. The mind and body cannot be separated. He says that for every physical problem, there is an emotional counterpart, which is usually found in a traumatic event in another incarnation.

While many people would be horrified by some of the things that they have done or that have happened to them in past lives, discovering these events can have a major impact on your present life. Finding out about negative past occurrences can release energies that cause severe physical and emotional problems in the present.

An effective approach to such physical and emotional problems is through hypnosis and past-life regression therapy. This enables you to search for the trauma that is creating a problem in this life. The trained hypnotist or regressionist gives instructions while you are under hypnosis on how to locate the past-life incident which caused or contributed to the present problem.

A phobia in your present life may be the result of the unconscious memory of a death in another incarnation. Deep depression may be viewed as frozen anger from a past incarnation. Working through these fear-based emotions to the point of complete forgiveness can open the path to the full expression and experiences of love to the final healing.

The behavior of my grandson supports my belief in reincarnation. We believe Josh is a reincarnation of his late grandfather, a railroad engineer who loved locomotives. When Josh was a tiny baby, his grandmother bought a painting of a locomotive and hung it on the nursery wall. Though he was less than a year old, Josh's delight for that picture was unmistakable. When his mother presented him with a toy train set, he was ecstatic! When he could barely put sentences together, he said, "Mommy, when I was up there," pointing upward, "I was my grandpa, but I decided to come down here and be your little boy."

Surely child prodigies are proof enough of past lives. Where else could they have achieved such knowledge if not in another life? How could Mozart compose complicated pieces of music before the age of five? How else does one explain Josef Hofmann, who played the piano expertly at the age of one-and-a-half?

There is the case of Rosemary Brown, an English medium who won fame as the purported channel for Liszt, Chopin, Beethoven, Brahms, Debussy, Schubert, Schumann, Bach, and others. They dictated to her, compositions from the spirit world. She had only a few piano lessons, and had no special training as a musician. As these great composers from the other world came to her, each she was able to memorize and play their compositions, expertly within twenty minutes.

The London Psychic News stated, "The phenomenon of Rosemary Brown's achievement presents a challenge... it cannot be dismissed by some facile explanation. Perhaps the deceased assemblage of the world's greatest composers is intended to demonstrate survival after death to dispel our doubt and fear of the afterlife."

Would you like to discover who you were in a past life? Remember that active memory is only a small part of normal waking consciousness, and that the subconscious mind registers every past impression and experience. You can tap those memories stored in your subconscious memory with this simple mirror technique, which will enable you to find out without hypnosis or past-life regression. You may also use this technique to explore the interims between lives.

One woman was surprised when she saw a man in the mirror. She had never thought about having been a man and she began to laugh. She said, "When I laughed, he just looked very sternly back at me. He did not think it was funny."

This exercise should be done in the same manner as your other metaphysical practices with proper breathing and relaxation techniques. Optimum results can be expected if this technique is used at night.

Technique To Discover Past Lives

1. Dim the lights or turn them out and sit in a comfortable chair in front of a mirror with a lighted candle to your left.

2. Focus on your breathing. Count the inhalations and exhalations. Relax more and more with each breath. Become completely one with the rhythms of your breath.

3. Keep your eyes half open and unfocused. Let your body go almost limp as you relax yourself completely.

4. Stare into the mirror, looking deep into your own eyes, thinking, "I want to know who I was in another life."

5. Your eyes will begin to tear. Keep your eyes focused on their reflection in the mirror.

6. The mirror will begin to shimmer. This means you are succeeding.

7. A picture will begin to emerge. The picture will become clearer. It might be just a face or it can be an actual happening from your past life that is reenacted. Sometimes a succession of past incarnations will appear.

CHAPTER ELEVEN

Communicating With The Dead

Have you ever wished you could communicate with someone who has already passed over? Perhaps you feel as if a loved one was taken from you too soon? You can communicate with these departed friends and loved ones, in fact, you may already have.

One of the most exciting aspects of my work is the phenomenon of communicating with the dead. I have witnessed a great deal of phenomenon concerning the death experience. Many years of metaphysical study and training have taught me that indeed there are duplicate worlds, the visible and the invisible; the physical and the astral. I understand that there is no death as we know it but rather a new dimension far more splendid than anything on earth.

The Eastern world view concerning death—the laws of karma and reincarnation—teach us that death is not an ending. It is a continual process of learning and rebirth. We are constantly advancing to a higher realm of consciousness with each new life cycle.

Even in our own western culture the promise of heavenly love is revealed in the retelling of death experiences and the glorious tunnel of light that awaits us on the other side. Death is a beginning. It is an advancement toward knowledge and light. So why then is the idea of death; our own and others, such a cause of pain and fear?

Much of the pain we feel when we lose someone we love centers around our inability to exchange words and ideas with the person who has passed on. We cannot, for example, pick up the phone and ask them where they are, are they alright, are they afraid?

To continue to communicate with those who are no longer in this dimension you must learn to hear and speak in new ways. You must learn to trust your feelings and intuitions. It is not unusual to dream of a loved one, a grandmother or a friend , only to hear soon after that they died on the very day they appeared in the dream. Departed loved ones are communicating with us all the time!

Here is the story of how my daughter contacted me after her death. It was the day of the funeral; Debbie was only eighteen years old when she died. I wondered how we could go on without her. If only I didn't have to see her in that coffin, looking so thin and old from the ravages of terminal cancer! I thought my legs would crumble beneath me as I made my way to the funeral home.

As I entered, I noticed there were lots of people chatting quietly. Everyone in the room was paying their respects to Debbie and sharing stories of what a wonderful person she had been. But knowing she was so loved by her classmates and their families was small comfort. My daughter was gone and my heart was breaking!

As I started across the room toward the casket, I heard a very familiar sound. I heard Debbie giggle! She always giggled a lot. I looked up toward the ceiling in the direction of her voice. I didn't see her but at that moment she said loudly, "Mom, surely you don't think that is *me*, in that coffin, do you?"

"Debbie?"

I looked around the room hoping for signs that other people had heard her voice. It was obvious that no one in the room had heard her but me. I decided I must be delirious from grief. I wasn't ready to accept that what I had experienced was real. Over the years I have developed my psychic abilities to help others in times of need, but in my own life, I was ready to dispel this communique from my daughter as a grief induced hallucination! I was ready to believe I had simply imagined the whole thing.

I soon realized that hearing Debbie's laughter had a profound effect on me. A sense of calm came over me. All at once, I knew everything would be alright. It was as if her voice had released me from my grief. My sorrow vanished. This was not a hallucination but rather it was Debbie's way of letting me know she was alright.

Later, my other daughter went to the mortuary to pay her respects. When she returned home, she called me into her room.

"Mom," she said, "I think I am having a nervous breakdown. You know how much I loved Debbie. Her death has been too much for me, I guess!"

She proceeded to tell me that she had also heard Debbie's voice. Debbie had giggled and said the very same words to her.

"Am I having a nervous breakdown, Mom? Nobody in that room heard her but me, and Mom, it was loud! It felt so good to hear her voice again. It took all my pain away. How could my grief just vanish like that? I don't understand any of this."

"She said those very words to me. Then she giggled as she so often used to do. And my grief is also gone! I don't understand it, either, honey. It had to be Debbie's way of easing our pain," I answered.

My daughter confirmed it. Debbie's message was real. We have never felt that kind of grief concerning Debbie since then. Her laughter assured us that wherever she is, she is doing fine. Our minds are at ease knowing she is alright.

Here is a simple technique for communicating with a loved one who has already passed over. It involves psychometry; using an object that once belonged to the person you are trying to contact. Choose a piece of jewelry or an item of clothing. Make sure that the object you use is something the person enjoyed and had good feelings about. This technique should be done after breathing and relaxation exercises to rid your mind of any distractions.

Sit in a comfortable chair with a notebook and pen nearby for note taking later. After you have finished your breathing and relaxation exercises, visualize your entire body being surrounded by a clear, colorless light. See the light cover your body with a shield of positive protective energy.

Begin to fill your mind with pictures of the person you are trying to contact. See them at their best moments. Imagine their face, their eyes, how they walked and talked. It is important to create a vivid and dynamic picture of the person in your mind so that you can see the life forces working within them.

Hold the object in your hand. Images will instantly begin to appear. Do not try to control these images. Allow your subconscious to take them in. Remember, your subconscious will record every detail. You may begin to hear words. It may feel at first as if you are making them up but do not question the messages. Just allow your subconscious to remember everything.

When you are finished place the object on a table nearby and begin to write down your impressions. What did you see and hear? Do not edit what you write, just get it all down on paper. Only once you have finished should you begin to try to interpret what you've written. It is very important that you do not second guess the messages you receive. These messages come in various forms and sometimes you get them when least expected.

Just after my brother died I received such a message. Many years ago Jim and I made a pact. Whichever one of us died first, that one would come back and communicate from the other side. Jim has made some memorable visits since his death.

One day, I was walking through the living room when a book came flying out of nowhere. The book landed in my path right where I was about to step and the pages of the book were open. I picked it up and read the passage. It was all about "life after death." This same thing happened again about two days later with another book, and it contained the same message.

My brother's wrist watch is a mystery. It chimes every night at the hour of his death. We have never replaced the batteries, yet the little chimes fill the room every night at 1:15 a.m. I could have chosen to view all these things as coincidence. Gravity causes objects to fall; watches have built in alarms; perfectly reasonable explanations, right? I could have chosen to ignore the fact that my brother made a promise: he would contact me after his death. I chose instead to see the truth. My brother Jim has made contact.

Mystical experiences come in many forms. They may seem like dreams. But these happenings are real. You need to learn to trust that what you've experienced is not just your imagination. I had this strange vision or out of body experience where I actually argued with a presence who seemed to be a messenger; an angel of death; a Gabriel. I am quite certain I was not asleep. I know it was not a dream. The visual experience had all the qualities of a real-life happening.

I could see clearly the golden halo around his head and his luminous white robe; even the varied shades of white on his wings. I remember looking out the window and seeing billowy white clouds against a blue sky.

I was standing in the kitchen when he suddenly appeared before me. I was conscious of the light green breakfast nook, the white appliances, and the multicolored tile on the floor. I could see and identify all the different colors in the room. It was not a dream.

We stood by the window as he announced, "I have come for you."

Looking him straight in the eye, I answered, "That's too bad. I am not going anywhere with you. My children need me."

"You don't seem to understand. This is not debatable, nor is it a request."

"Oh, I understand alright, but I am NOT going with you," I answered assertively.

"You have no say in the matter," he responded.

"Look here, I have at least ten good years left in this body and I intend to use every last one of them!"

"Just what am I supposed to tell them up there? How in

the world will I explain this failure to complete my task?" he muttered.

"That is not my concern. My interest is in living to raise my children and I must finish that job," I answered.

I watched as he left; walking higher and higher with each step. He was shaking his head and muttering to himself. Whatever he told them up there must have registered because what happened next changed my life forever. It would prove, beyond a doubt, that I had been sent for—it was not a dream.

The Death Experience

Death is a mystery. Most of us cannot predict what *life after death* will be like. We can only hope that our soul continues on with peace and light, but the true nature of death can only be revealed to us as it actually happens.

In 1985 it happened to me. I became ill and had to undergo dangerous surgery. My doctor was very candid about the risks involved and I knew when I went to the hospital that I might not survive. My husband and I had to prepare for whatever lay ahead.

I was very happily married with two small children and I could not bare to think that I might be taken away from my family. How could my husband ever handle a situation of this magnitude? How could he raise two small children alone? My family was my heaven on earth! Was I to miss their triumphs?...their achievments?...and their hard learned mistakes?

I died on the operating table.

Nothing in my years of metaphysical work prepared me for the incredible wonder of Divine Love. I was suddenly encompassed by a beautiful luminous light. It was warm and full of love. I could feel my spirit being released from my body as I began to float. I was light as a feather, floating upward, weightless. It was as if the prison which I had cherished as my body was no more. I was free as the air; no encumbrances.

As I drifted up, toward this pure white light, I felt myself becoming one with the luminescence. I was nothing yet I was becoming part of all there is.

I always knew that the Divine One, Universal Intelligence, whatever one chooses to call the "Almighty Presence" is portrayed as light. I thought, "So this is what is meant by 'We return to the Godhead from which we came.'"

There are no words in the English language that truly describe the euphoria and love I felt as I left my body. It was so beautiful and satisfying that for the first time I did not think of my husband and the children I was leaving behind. I was home! There was no thought of anything except absolute euphoria!

But I was not meant to stay in that realm of light and love for very long. I was brought back. It was clear. I had spoken with the messenger and had refused to go with him. Weeks prior to my operation I had decided that I was not ready to die. It had been no dream.

Once I had recovered though, I became very depressed. During my death experience, the warmth and love I had felt was so compelling, I would rather have stayed on the other side. It is hard for people to understand unless they have experienced it for themselves. What I had considered to be my "heaven-on-earth"—the love of my family—was little in comparison to the unconditional love I experienced in death.

Life would never be the same. I soon realized why I was brought back. My psychic abilities grew quite strong, especially in the field of clairvoyance and healing. I was to use these new abilities to help others. I have since had so many strange happenings in my life; there is almost nothing too hard to believe.

Death is not to be feared. It is instead a time of great comfort and light. Many of us have an overwhelming *fear* of death. Our culture has provided us with an astounding number of negative associations to death; the haunted grave-yard, etc. Is it any wonder we're afraid of what death might be like?

If, like so many of us, you fear for any loved ones who have already crossed over, there is a very simple technique you can use to communicate with them. Ask them to come to you in your dreams.

Before going to sleep take a few deep breaths, relaxing more and more with each breath. Keep your eyes closed and keep breathing. With each breath notice that you are becoming increasingly heavy all over. Continue to focus on your breathing. Your head becomes weighty on the pillow. Your eyes are heavy. You want to go to sleep but you must not allow sleep yet.

You feel a deep heaviness all over. Your breathing becomes deeper and deeper. A vague dreaminess sweeps over you. You are now in the hypnogogic state. Everything is far, far away. All tension is gone. You have blocked everything from your mind.

Begin to say these words over and over. "I will dream of ———." You don't need to say these words out loud but you must continue to repeat them in your head. "Tonight, I will dream of ———. I will dream of ———. Tonight I will dream of ———. I will dream of ———."

Eventually you will fall deeper into the theta frequency

and eventually you will drift into sleep. Make sure you leave a note pad and pen by the bedside for note taking in the morning.

Your dream experience can be very useful in easing any sorrow or pain you have over the loss of a loved one. There are many ways to learn about the death experience: astral travel, past-life regression, communicating with earthbound spirits. All of these techniques, if used properly, help to reconnect you to someone who is no longer in our every day world.

Technique For Communicating With A Loved One: Psychometry

1. Choose an object that belonged to the person you are trying to contact.

2. Sit in a comfortable chair. Place a notebook and pen nearby.

3. Clear your mind and focus on your breathing. Breathe in to the count of five. Breathe out to the count of seven. Relax completely.

4. Visualize a clear, protective light as it surrounds your entire body.

5. Begin to fill your mind with vivid and dynamic pictures of the person you are trying to contact.

6. Hold the object in your hand. Images will begin to appear. Words will begin to form in your head. Your subconscious will record every detail. Just allow all the impressions to come to you— **do not edit them!**

7. When you are finished, write down all your impressions. Your subconscious has remembered them all.

Technique For Communicating With The Dead: Dreams

1. Place a pen and notepad nearby and lie in bed.

2. Focus on your breathing and relax completely.

3. Feel very sleepy...feel a deep heaviness all over.

4. Don't go to sleep, just let yourself relax completely.

5. Begin to say these words, "I will dream of —
———. Tonight I will dream of———." Continue to repeat these words over and over until you drift into sleep. You do not have to speak these words aloud.

6. Take notes as soon as possible upon waking.

In summary, if you should feel the presence of the spirit of a loved one, don't be alarmed. There is no such thing as death, as we know it. Life is a continual process and it never ends. This is what eternity is. If you should have an out-of-body or death experience, you will never again fear death. Ask anyone who has been blessed with the phenomenon.

About the Author

Audrey Craft Davis has a master's degree in metaphysics and has earned doctorate degrees in divinity and psychology. Davis is an author, lecturer, entrepreneur, and a veteran teacher and counselor. She is currently immersed in three other book projects and has authored numerous magazine articles. Her poetry book *Pathways* has received twelve merits of award. She is included in *Who's Who In American Education* as well as in *The Registrar of Honors*, Cambridge, England.

Audrey has set up motivational programs and women's groups as well as many other public service programs. Davis can be reached at 8039 Garden Drive #204, Seminole, FL 34647.

FREE MAGAZINE

Dick and Tara Sutphen publish a quarterly magazine that is mailed to 200,000 book/tape buyers and seminar attendees. A sample issue is free, and if you purchase or attend a seminar, the publication is mailed free for two years. If you purchased this book in a bookstore, send the receipt (or a copy) and we'll add you to the mailing list for two years.

Each issue is approximately 80 pages and contains news, research reports and articles on metaphysics, psychic exploration and self-help, in addition to providing information on Sutphen Seminars, and 300 audio and video tapes: hypnosis, meditation, sleep programming, subliminal programming and inner-harmony music.

Books From Valley of the Sun

Ultra-Depth Hypnosis

Audio/Video Tapes That Relate To This Book
Available Through Your Local Metaphysical Bookseller
Or Directly From Valley of the Sun Publishing

RX17® Audio Programming

Side A: Hypnosis. **Side B:** Subliminal suggestions hidden in soothing music. One hour. Boxed in slip case.

**Chakra Balancing
RX203—$14.98**

**Higher-Self
Altered State Explorations
RX205—$14.98**

Dream Solutions RX106—$14.98

2-Tape Albums

Contains 2 audio cassette tapes & Instruction Manual.

**Past-Life Therapy
AX901—$24.98**

**Rapidly Develop Psychic Ability
C837—$24.98**

Video Hypnosis®

4 kinds of mind programming, including subliminal audio and video. Thirty minutes, VHS only.

**Chakra Balancing
VHS109—$24.98**

**Past-Life Regression
VHS129—$24.98**

**Positive Thinking
VHS119—$24.98**

Tara Sutphen Meditations

Beautiful guided meditations to explore your life and find answers. 1 hour.

**Automatic Writing
TS205—$11.98**

**Spirit Guide Meditation
TS206—$11.98**

CD Meditation Journeys

A unique new kind of meditation journey with 3-D sound. The story processes you as you explore. Over an hour, on CD.

Temple of Light CD777—$16.98

Gateless Gate CD778—$16.98

Audio Workshop

Contains all the training you need to become a good hypnosis subject.

**How To Be A Better Receiver In Hypnosis
NX502—$14.98**